MW00628497

GENTLEMEN,
START YOUR ENGINES!

GENTLEMEN, START YOUR ENGINES!

Dr. Bob Moorehead

Overlake Christian Press
Kirkland, Washington

© 1995 by Dr. Bob Moorehead
All rights reserved. Published March, 1995.

No part of this publication may be reproduced, stored in a retrieval
system, or transmitted in any form by any means, electronic, mechanical,
photocopy, recording, or otherwise, without the prior written permission
of the publisher except for brief quotations in critical reviews or articles.

Unless otherwise noted, the Bible version used in this publication is The
Holy Bible: New International Version. Copyright © 1973, 1978, 1984
International Bible Society. Used by permission of Zondervan Bible
Publishers.

Lyrics from *Cat's In The Cradle* on page 130 © 1974 STORY SONGS,
LTD. Used with permission. All rights reserved.

Overlake Christian Press
9051 132nd Avenue N.E., Kirkland, Washington 98033

Printed in the United States of America.

ISBN 0-9639496-3-2

This book is dedicated to the late Ed Towne, pastor, friend, mentor and colleague, who loved me, encouraged me and was caring enough to ask the right questions. He was taken to be with the Lord just three hours before he was to preach, March 8, 1992 at age 44.

CONTENTS

FOREWORD

Between the green flag (beginning of the book) and the checkered flag (end of the book), there is generally a race to be run and won. If you race through this book (scan it), you will want to make sure your mental VCR (memory) is turned on afterward. You will want to rewind it in slow motion to be able to enjoy every turn on the track of truth.

Bob has taken his years of ministry, personal living, and both theological and practical training, and put them into this one volume of easily readable material for men. It is rich and rewarding in its application of knowledge.

Just as soap is without purpose until applied, so is truth.

His definitions, listings, and outlines for easy understanding, the ability to "see" what is meant, are stuff that you want to copy and carry with you, paste on your mirror, and most of all have written on the tablets of your heart and mind.

Both Germany and Russia after World Wars I and II, became known as "fatherless" because of the incredible loss of men's lives during the wars. America is becoming "fatherless" through the loss of responsibility in the lives of its men.

The new wave of God's Spirit that is sweeping the nation, and the world, is to bring men both to their senses and their knees. Prior to this generation the previous two or three emphasized children, youth and women.

Beginning just over a decade ago the emphasis began to change toward men. We began to realize that you could develop preventive programs for children, rehabilitation programs for youth in need, cultural development programs for women, but when they all went back home they had the same problems with the man.

Now change is coming where it has always needed to start - with the man. "A father's responsibility is not to make his children's decisions for them, but to let them see him make his (excerpt from *Real Man*)."

Once you have read and studied this book, read it with your wife, and then with your family.

Adding his voice and weight of influence through his wisdom and experience, Bob Moorehead is making it impossible for men to plead ignorance as an excuse for maturation failure. With this book he gives no place for the "Peter Pan Syndrome," immature males in men's bodies, to exist.

"Start Your Engines" is a euphemism for "grow up!"

Dr. Edwin Cole

INTRODUCTION

Every book begins somewhere! This book actually began while my wife and I were on a tour of the Daytona International Speedway in Daytona Beach, Florida. I figured we would probably never see the Daytona 500, so this was the next best thing. We were shown pictures of the early days when racing was on the beach, then given the history of the present race track and its development. We were taken to the mechanic's pit area, the check-in area, the first-aid area, the warm-up bay, and finally the track itself, where people drive cars at speeds of over 200 miles per hour.

Then we had an unexpected treat. Our tour group got to go into the over 92,000-seat stands and then they turned on a high definition disk of an actual race, simulating parts for brevity. But the part that brought chills to me was when the announcer said, GENTLEMEN, START YOUR ENGINES! We then heard a deafening roar of those high-powered engines, and we heard the race begin. The disk had also recorded the crowd on race day, and we felt as if "we were there."

When we left that massive race track, one thing kept repeating itself in my mind. Right. You guessed it. GENTLEMEN, START YOUR ENGINES.

I told my wife as we drove to the beach that day, "That's what the men of America need to do more than anything else, START THEIR ENGINES."   It's time for men to be men again, to take back their masculinity, their sense of chivalry, their leadership, their manliness. It's time for the men of this country to be men, real men, reclaiming their "place" in the home, the shop, city hall, the church, and the community as a whole. So much in so short a time has been abrogated to someone else. No, I'm not a male chauvinist, nor am I one who believes that men are superior to women, but it's time that an appreciation for the differences was restored. I believe the men in our country have cheated the women with a "unisex" philosophy, erasing all respect for the God-given differences with which men and women were endowed.

This book deals with the major areas of a man's life in which he struggles to some degree. It deals with man the husband, man the neighbor, man the employee, man the thinker, man the dreamer, and man the father and pace-setter. The average American male changes hats several times a week, sometimes not so gracefully. He struggles as much or more than his female counterpart with his role and how he is seen by his peers.

In the weakness department, men have some common denominators. We will discuss those. Men come in all shapes and sizes; short, tall, fat, skinny, muscular, puny; he has red hair, black hair, blonde hair, brown hair, and no hair. He can rise to the occasion so that his whole family is very proud. He can also make a complete fool of himself at his son's Little League game. He can be a shining example to his 16-

year-old son of virtue, honesty, and by being a law-abiding citizen...until he gets a speeding ticket with his son in the car! He can make his wife so proud when he "makes the big sale" and his company is pleased; but he's lower than a snake's belly when he comes home and shows her his pink slip.

If you've read this, and you are a man who has your act totally together, then this book is not for you, give it to your neighbor! If you never fly off the handle, have all of your lusts under control, are a model husband and father, have no stress from work, have plenty of money left over from pay check to pay check, you're a spiritual giant, and never feel frustrated about anything, and your wife finds absolutely no faults in you, then you've bought the wrong book, or if someone gave this to you, give it back and tell them you don't need it!

If, on the other hand, you sometimes find yourself in a rut, you often lack courage, you are tempted by strong lusts, you feel you lose your direction in life occasionally, then read on...you're my kind of man, and I've written about you in the following pages.

You might find yourself as you read saying, "that guy's been reading my mail, my mind, and my secret desires." No, I really haven't, I just know a lot about men...I am one.

So, GENTLEMEN...START YOUR ENGINES, IT'S TIME TO GO!!

Finally, be strong in the Lord and in his mighty power (Ephesians 6:10).

1

KEEP THAT BATTERY CHARGED

A Man and His Spiritual Development

Once I read about an experienced race car driver who had qualified for a race with a handsome purse. He had spent the week polishing his car, making sure the tires were the best and were inflated properly, that the radiator was full, and that the oil was changed. The day of the race came. Everything seemed ready. When the race master said "Gentlemen, start your engines," he turned his key! Instead of hearing the roar of his engine he heard that dreaded sound, "roar-ur-roar-ur-roar-ur" getting weaker and weaker. His battery was dead! He thought he had thought of everything, but he had failed to put the charger on the night before to make sure he had plenty of juice. He had the finest engine that could be bought, the best and safest frame a race car could possibly have, but with no power to ignite the engine and run the car, he was "dead on the track."

Men, especially, are subject to "dead batteries." I'm not talking about the ones with cables that go in a car, I'm talking about the inner power that keeps them going. A man can have a well proportioned body, biceps perfect, a flat tummy and large chest, but if his power supply is dead, he won't get anywhere. I'm talking about the spiritual resources within that enable us to cope, be creative, be victorious, and be winners.

Man looks at the outward appearance, But God looks at the heart (1 Samuel 16:7).

Men jog to be successful in their health, they dress to be successful in their business, they eat to be successful in their looks, but many times they will neglect and ignore their other dimension, the inner, spiritual man.

Paul reminded us of the danger of becoming so caught up with our material and physical well being that we forget the most important part:

Physical training is of some value, but godliness has value for all things, holding promise for the present life and the life to come (I Timothy 4:8).

He's saying that we need to take care of our health, our bodies, our looks; but it's really more important that we develop godliness in our lives.

Of course, spiritual development is predicated on the fact that there is something to develop! I'm saying that birth is first, then growth and development. If you have never received Jesus Christ as your Savior, and committed your life to Him, then there is nothing to develop. The Bible teaches us that we're all born with the stain of sin on us. It further teaches that we cannot remove that sinful stain.

Although you wash yourself with soda and use an abundance of soap, the stain of your guilt is still before me...(Jeremiah 2:22).

Man, in his depravity, is totally incapable of doing anything about his condition as a sinner. It will take the intervention of God. That's why in order to be saved, the first thing we need to admit is that we're sinners, and that we cannot do anything about that condition ourselves. This news is a low blow to men who think they're invincible and can do anything. The fact is, the Bible says that the way of man is not in himself.

I know, O Lord, that a man's life is not his own; it is not for man to direct his steps (Jeremiah 10:23).

Left to himself, man can make a mess of things, especially his own life! We need the Lord in our life...desperately!

If you have never personally invited Jesus Christ into your heart, it isn't complicated. The Bible says that we're to repent of sin. That is to decide to change directions and forsake all known sin, and turn to the Lord. Acts 3:19 commands us to repent so that times of refreshing may come from the presence of the Lord.

Next, we need to confess Jesus Christ as God and Savior, that He's the Lord of our life. Romans 10:9,10 tell us if we do that, we'll be saved. If you have never done that, you may put this book down long enough to pray the following prayer:

Lord, I know I'm a sinner. I'm truly sorry for my sins. I believe that you, Lord Jesus, died for me on the cross and rose on the third day. I confess you to be my Savior and Lord, come into my life right now! Amen.

Good, now that He's THERE, it's up to you to grow in that special relationship you have with Him. The best way to do that is to develop your spiritual life, so that your battery will always be charged. The best way to do that is to have a daily quiet time, just you and the Lord.

STEPS TO A DAILY BATTERY CHARGE

1. Be convinced of the need

Just as a drunk can never be cured until he wants sobriety like a drowning man wants air, you cannot have a successful daily quiet time until you are convinced that this is absolutely necessary, not just a good thing to do.

I'm a living example of the necessity of a daily time alone with God. I was into my ministry only a few years, with only a "hit and miss" prayer time, when I heard a devotional, by a coach, at a breakfast one morning. He used only one scripture, but it's been indelibly etched on my heart ever since.

> Very early in the morning: while it was still dark, Jesus got up, left the house and went off to a solitary place, where he prayed (Mark 1:35).

Your elevator doesn't have to go all the way to the top to realize that if Jesus, the divine Son of God, the incarnate Deity, sinless in every way, sensed the need to get alone with God on a regular basis, who do we think that we are that we can survive spiritually without the same practice?

The Bible says that Jesus has called us his friends (John 15:15). One mark of true friendship is that friends love to get together, walk together, talk together, and just be together. A time set aside to get into God's Word and let it speak to me, and a time to pour my heart out to God, is absolutely necessary if I'm going to live the Christian life successfully. It will spell the difference between existing and living.

So before you go any further, settle in your own mind that this time is totally necessary to keep your batteries charged so your life can run.

2. Determine The Time

I've never really met a man that told me he had time on his hands. Everybody's busy. Someone said we're so busy we're "honking at our own tail lights!" Thinking that a great big block of time is going to just drop down out of the sky, for you to get into God's Word and pray, is not very realistic. I found in my own life that I had to clear my schedule, make the time, and give it as high a priority as my time to eat or take a shower.

I realize you can't get legalistic about what time of day you go into seclusion for prayer and the Word, but I've found out that if you don't do it in the morning before you go to work, it's likely you won't do it at all. Once the phones, the fax, the e-mail, and the interruptions begin, the likelihood of finding time during the day is greatly diminished. By the time you get home in the evening and attempt to spend time with your wife and family, the evening zings by pretty rapidly. At bedtime your brain and body are extremely tired. The best time is early in the morning before life has had a chance to groove anything on your brain.

Starting each day with God's Word and God's presence colors the decisions and reactions you make throughout the day. You may need to resist the temptation to read the sports page or the business section of the paper, to make a priority of hearing from God, but believe me, it will be worth it.

3. Determine The Place

This may sound elementary, but I've found that every man needs to seek out a place to be alone with God. Jesus did and we need to do the same. Jesus went to a solitary place. It really doesn't matter where you go as long as it is...

- A consistent place
- A distraction-free place
- A conducive place to pray
- A comfortable place

It could be a closet, a back yard, a deck, a living room, your bathroom, but make sure you won't be interrupted there, because you're in communion with God. It needs to be a place where passers-by aren't looking, so that if you want to lie prostrate or stand with uplifted hands in worship, you may.

4. Determine A Definite Plan

Not to over-organize, but since we usually only have an hour or less, we need to make the most of it. I've found the following plan to be helpful.

Practice the presence of God. Take a few minutes before reading scripture just to affirm God's presence. I usually say, "Lord I know You're here, help me just now to experience Your closeness."

Read at least one chapter from the Old Testament. A good starting place is Psalms. If the Psalm is short, you may want to read two or three. Some like to read the chapter each day in Proverbs that matches the day of the month.

Read one of the growth chapters of the New Testament every day for one week. Some of those chapters are: Matthew 5-7; Luke 6; John 6, 10, 15; Galatians 5, 6; Romans 12; 1 Corinthians 15; 2 Corinthians 4, 5, 8; Ephesians 4-6; Philippians 2, 4; Colossians 3; I Peter 5; 2 Peter 3; Hebrews 11-13; or all of I John. It's usually helpful to try to memorize one chapter a month in the New Testament.

Spend the rest of the time in prayer. Everyone has a pattern of prayer that is meaningful to them. If you don't happen to have one, I'll share the one that is meaningful to me.

- Adoration and Praise (praise God, sing to Him if you can)
- Thanksgiving - make a thanks list, and thank God

for all His provision.
- Confession - Confess your sins according I John 1:9
- Intercession and petition
- Claiming God's answers and agreeing in faith.

Sometimes it's good just to sit and think about God, His greatness, His attributes. He is:

- Jehovah-Jireh, Our provider
- Jehovah-Nissi, Our banner
- Jehovah-Rophi, Our healer
- Jehovah-Rohi, Our shepherd
- Jehovah-Tsidkinu, Our righteousness

Most men, being basically task-oriented, find it hard to come before the God who says:

Be still, and know that I am God (Psalm 46:10).

Daily quiet times don't come easily for us men, not even for pastors. This discipline has to be cultivated. The repeated "renewing of the mind" will take you from babyhood, into adolescence, and on to adulthood spiritually. How is the mind renewed? Wouldn't it be wonderful just to lift the mind out at night and soak it in bleach, then put it back in the morning? But there's something even better than that! It's allowing God's Word to renew your mind.

...Be transformed by the renewing of your mind (Romans 12:2).

...Be made new in the attitude of your minds (Ephesians 4:23).

...Put on the new self, which is being renewed in knowledge in the image of its Creator (Colossians 3:10).

This is done by passing scripture through the sieve of our mind. Men, we will not make it without God's Word dwelling in us richly daily (Colossians 3:16). The degree to which we are in God's Word will be the degree to which we are victorious over sin. That's why the Psalmist said:

I have hidden your word in my heart that I might not sin against you (Psalm 119:11).

How can a young man keep his way pure? By living according to your word (Psalm 119:9).

So, don't get caught with a dead battery! You won't if you keep it charged daily with your own spiritual development.

I hope you're on your way!

2

WHAT'S UNDER THE HOOD?

The Difference Between Men and Women

In walking through the museum of racing at the Daytona International Speedway, I noticed pictures of the victory wreaths being placed over the winners. One of the pictures showed a winner with the hood of his car open. The caption showed him saying, "VICTORS KNOW WHAT'S UNDER THEIR HOOD!" I'll bet that's right!

It doesn't matter what the outward cosmetics are on the car of a winner. It doesn't matter whether it has whitewall or black tires, or whether its paint is blue metallic or candy-apple red. It all comes down to what's under the hood.

Men are strange, unique, and sometimes weird creatures. If you don't believe me, look under their hood...at what makes them tick. It's what's under the hood that counts, so it needs to be the right thing!

A few years ago I met a young man in our church who had married only three weeks earlier. "How's married life?"

I asked him. "Wonderful, wonderful, wonderful," he said with a big smile on his face. Then he put his hand to his mouth and whispered in my ear, "Women are really different from men, aren't they?" I heard him! I knew what he was talking about. I needed no interpreter. He was not prepared for the fact that men are wired differently than women — mentally, emotionally, and in many other ways.

My experience has revealed some basic differences between a man and a woman. Let me show you some of these basic differences:

MAN	WOMAN
Fulfilled by job	Fulfilled by family
High energy level	Low energy level
Beauty = Function	Beauty = Aesthetics
Decisions by reason	Decisions by emotion
Verbal skills - Low	Verbal skills - High
Task oriented (doer)	Concept oriented (be-er)
Romance = Sex	Romance = Tenderness/sex
Basically non-trusting	Mostly trusting
Goal oriented	Relationship oriented
High risk-taker	Low risk-taker
Low discernment	High discernment
High schedule person	Low schedule person
Result oriented	Process oriented
Quick with decisions	Slow with decisions

I fully realize that no list is perfect. I realize that some women are goal oriented, even more so than their husbands. But by and large, the above basic-difference chart often rings true.

When a man lifts the hood and takes a good hard look at what is there (inside him), one thing he discovers for sure...he is very different from his female counterpart! These differences are not liabilities. After all, God made us different for good reasons. Unless we know the differences, acknowledge them, then learn to live within their context, our relationship with the opposite sex will be strained, to say the least.

I remember seeing Rick again in the hallway at church after about three months. "Well, how is married life?" I asked him. His response caught me off guard just a bit. "Why didn't someone tell me how different men and women are?" I smiled and said, "Welcome to reality!" My words were not much comfort, as Rick divulged to me how in only three months they had disagreed on more things than they could agree upon. Most of their arguments centered around one thing. Neither of them had been told how sharp the differences are that exist between male and female.

Here are just a few areas where those differences are prominent.

ENERGY

Generally, a male can take more, last longer, and tire more slowly than a female when it comes to expending energy. It's not just a hormonal difference, but a temperament difference. Because men tend to be task and goal oriented, they go about their work with much more gusto and abandon than most women. They are apt to work far beyond the time they begin to get tired. A woman might tend to quit for a while when she begins to tire. I know a man who comes home from work about 5:30, jogs three miles, plays two sets of tennis, mows his lawn, and then putters in his workshop before retiring! Many women, whether they work outside the home or inside, begin to run out of steam about five or six o'clock in the evening. The energy just isn't there. If a husband does not realize that his wife doesn't feel like doing something extra in the evening, or is not energetic toward sex at ten o'clock, it can cause some real conflict.

FULFILLMENT

The source of fulfillment in males and females differs drastically. Because most males are competitive in nature, they find great fulfillment in their jobs, going toe-to-toe with the competition, closing a deal, making a sale, beating out the competition. A woman's fulfillment usually comes from her husband, her family, the decor of the house, perhaps even from hobbies like ceramics, cross stitch, or gardening. In other words, totally different areas bring a woman and a man to life. Going into and staying in a marriage without knowing that can be a real challenge.

BEAUTY

What is beautiful to a woman and what is beautiful to a man is totally different 99 percent of the time! I remember a couple in our church years ago. George was a steel and structural engineer. He got his jollies from taking his wife to a skyscraper, that he was overseeing during construction, two or three times a week. He would ooh and ahh over the symmetry of the building saying, "Isn't it beautiful how perfectly those pieces of steel come together on the corners?" He would recite the mathematical formulas that made a 38-floor skyscraper possible. He never understood why his wife did not share or understand his excitement!

Women, on the other hand, see beauty in aesthetics, such as art, flowers, mountain peaks or even clothing. She might ooh and aah about the color-coordination of a well-dressed person. Most men are oblivious to what matches and doesn't in clothes (many couldn't care less)!

Decision Making

Carl and Mary were house-shopping. They found a home with about 2,200 square feet that included a workshop just off the garage. Carl said, "This is it, let's buy it!" That same day they went through a house of identical square footage with no workshop, but $30,000 higher!

Mary wanted that house because out the kitchen window was a view of Mt. Rainier. Carl was thinking about making things to sell in the workshop. Mary was thinking of how good that mountain would make her feel while washing dishes. You can guess which house they bought! They saw a lot of Mt. Rainier after moving in!

He was thinking practically, while she was thinking aesthetically. Most men make decisions based on facts and pragmatism. Most women make decisions based on aesthetic perceptions and emotions. When a couple goes to buy a new car, the husband is interested more often in the tires, and engine's horsepower. The wife is likely to be interested in the texture and color of the interior. One decision is based on logic and reason, the other largely on feelings.

SEXUAL

Here is perhaps the greatest difference of all. Sexual needs differ vastly in women and men. They differ as well in how those needs are met. The height and thrill for a man in this area is sexual intercourse and his climax. He arrives at that much more quickly than the woman, as you know if you're married. A woman's need here is for intimacy. Intimacy for a man begins in bed. Intimacy for a woman begins hours before when she gets a bouquet of flowers from her husband, or a hug, a wink, or a caress in the kitchen. Just having her husband hold her, squeeze her, and whisper "I love you" can be just as exhilarating as the sexual act is for the man.

This does not mean sex isn't important to the woman. It is. But it may not hold the prominent place it does for the man. When the sexual act is over, the man's affections may cool very quickly, while the woman still needs to be held, caressed, and told that she is loved.

Someone has said that a woman needs love, so she has sex to get it from her husband. The husband needs sex, so he expresses love to get it. A woman needs love, and gives sex to get it; a man needs sex, so he gives love to get it.

Remember Rick? Married only three months, and very frustrated? Rick could not understand why he couldn't come home from work on his lunch hour, and in fifteen minutes make love to his wife, then return to work. For him it was a fairly mechanical operation. For his wife, it was a total exercise in futility! Why? Rick needed release from physical sexual pressure, and she needed romance. There was plenty of time to get the release in 15 or 20 minutes, but not enough time for her to get the romance and affection needed.

DOERS AND BE-ERS

There are many differences between male and female besides the obvious physical differences. A relationship cannot be built and sustained only on the physical relationship, as important as that is. Men are basically "doers" while women are basically "be-ers." This does not mean women are lazy. It just describes their nature.

A man would rather mow the lawn than take in an exhibit at the art gallery. He would rather change the oil and tune the engine in his car than choose the wallpaper for the kitchen. Most men don't enjoy window shopping, because it doesn't accomplish anything.

When a couple has to drive from Seattle to Portland, the goal of the woman is to enjoy the scenery and have lunch on the way in a nice restaurant. The man's goal is to get there! His tendency will be to drive above the speed limit with no stops. Her goal might be to drive right at 55 miles per hour, pull in to the rest stop, stop at all the view points, and take pictures. While she enjoys the trip, he enjoys the arrival.

Gentlemen, "Start Your Engines" by first checking to see what is under your hood (inside you). You'll enjoy the race much more!

3

DRIVING WITH CONFIDENCE

A Man and His Convictions

I was reading about the thickness, the durability, and the correct treading of the tires they put on race cars that travel in speeds of over 150 miles per hour. A race car enthusiast commented, "The tires are the very foundation of the race car. They spell the difference between crashing and running, winners and losers, life and death. As go the tires, so goes the race!" I then realized that champions don't skimp on the rubber! What tires are to the race car, convictions are to the man!

It was spring break and cars were bumper to bumper on the beach. Wild rock music was pouring out of the boom boxes on the cars. In most cases all you could hear was the heavy beat of the "boom, boom, boom, boom..." but I picked up some lyrics (actually so did everyone who was on the beach that day and maybe even those two continents away)! This is what I remember of the song:

> *Don't you know Mr. Joe, don't you know? You gotta go with the flow, Mr. Joe, just the flow; So, lay low, Mr.*

*Joe, lay low...Play it cool is the rule, status quo, Mr. Joe,
status quo! Be hip...don't rock the ship...Cause you know
Mr. Joe, yes you know Mr. Joe...you gotta go with the
flow, just go with the flow!"*

Doesn't that just grab you? I don't know who Mr. Joe
is, but if he takes the above advice, he isn't much of a
man! If there was ever a time men needed to buck the
flow, it's now. Whoever wrote the above lyrics is obviously a victim of a conviction-less, believe-nothing generation.

The Church, the culture, the nation, in fact our present
civilization is floundering today because men don't have
convictions. Boards of security and conviction we thought
were tightly nailed down are coming up. In the name of
being "politically correct" many men have sold out their
convictions for less than a mess of pottage. I firmly believe that somebody keeps moving the boundary lines. It's
called the shifting of the parameters. Nobody really does
"wrong" anymore. When they sin, they simply conve-
niently move the boundary line to accommodate their
lifestyle. What used to be called sexual perversion is now
called an "alternate lifestyle." Relabeling sin, calling it
something else, enables indulgers to go right on indulging
without fear of sanction or criticism.

There are some absolutes to life. It's not just nebulous
stuff that always changes. The Bible says:

By such things men live... (Isaiah 38:16).

God has given us some strong boundary lines, some
right paths, some truths that never change or go out of

style. Our generation needs the advice that another generation got 3,000 years ago from Jeremiah:

> *...stand at the crossroads and look; ask for the ancient paths, ask where the good way is, and walk in it, and you will find rest for your souls (Jeremiah 6:16b).*

I suppose everyone has some convictions, but the question is, what is their source? Some people's convictions cause them to make decisions on the basis of what is trendy, what is popular, what is the current and latest mood of the day. I recently talked to a father whose 18-year-old son brought his girlfriend over to spend the night, IN HIS BED! "You surely didn't allow it?" I asked. "Well," he responded, "it's a new day and people do those things today." I reminded him that his dad would have never allowed him to do that at 18 while he was still living in his house, and he concurred. "Do you know why your dad wouldn't allow it? Not because it was the 'in' thing to do, but because it was the right thing to do." If we cave in to what's popular, or the 'in' thing, we'll be changing our convictions like a chameleon changes colors.

Some people base their convictions by the line of least resistance. These people believe whatever is the easiest thing to believe. Their list of convictions are made up of those things that raise the least amount of controversy, cause least amount of flack, and will enable them to blend right in with the wallpaper! This is certainly a spineless method of arriving at one's convictions. These beliefs offend no one, raise no eyebrows, and will always be "politically and socially correct." They have a way of reducing a man to a wimp. They are not convictions based on absolute truth, but convictions based on the least amount of effort. It's "Mr. Joe, going with the flow."

Others base their convictions on what the majority is believing. I was in a fast food place recently filled with teenagers. One boy had the boldness to order a burger, fries, and medium coke (a creative order!). One by one the others in the group said, "make mine the same." I was waiting for some nonconformist to order fried grasshoppers and barbecued ostrich legs, but no one did! It was much easier just to order what everyone else was ordering.

Paul pleaded with the Romans:

> *Do not conform any longer to the pattern of this world...*
> *(Romans 12:2)*

I love the way J.B. Phillips has paraphrased that verse:

> *Don't let the world around you squeeze you into its*
> *mould... (J.B. Phillips translation)*

We're not called to be conformists, but world changers. In London's Highgate cemetery, chiseled on the tomb of Karl Marx are these words:

> *"The philosophers have only interpreted the world; the*
> *point is to change it!"*

How true those words are, especially from a Christian perspective. Some men base their convictions on what will get them ahead in business. The set of ethics they adopt are determined by what you have to do to turn a profit, make a sale, beat out the competitor. I read recently about a CEO in a plastics company. He was indicted by a grand jury for using a poor grade of resin in fasteners which he sold to the federal government. By making the fasteners with weaker materials, he was able to underbid all competitors, and thus got contract after contract...until he was discovered.

His response? "Well, you do what you have to do to turn a buck...competition is fierce." No remorse, no regret, no admission of wrong. He was adjusting his ethics to his practice, instead of the other way around.

It reminds me of some tourists who were driving through Arkansas. They saw dozens of pine trees with targets drawn on them, and a large hole right in the bull's eye. One hundred percent of the targets had holes right in the middle. They stopped for coffee in a small diner and saw a hillbilly with his rifle sitting at the counter.

"Are you the one who shot those trees and got a bull's eye every time?" "Yep, I'm the one," the old timer said with a sheepish smile. The tourists asked, "How on earth were you able to get a bull's eye 100 percent of the time?" The old timer smiled again and said, "Pretty easy, really, I shot the tree, then drew the target!" That may work in rural Arkansas with pine trees, but as a means of establishing convictions, it won't wash.

So, how do you establish convictions?

KNOW WHO YOU ARE IN CHRIST!

If you have accepted Jesus Christ as your Savior, you have become a somebody indeed. Listen to what Peter

wrote to Christian exiles who had been stripped of virtually every material possession:

> *But you are a chosen people, a royal priesthood, a holy*
> *nation, a people belonging to God...Once you were not*
> *a people, but now you are the people of God...(I Peter*
> *2:9a, 10a).*

When you stop and think about it, the Bible has
an impressive list of who we are in Christ.

Here are some:

- Children of God - Galatians 3:16
- His righteousness - 2 Corinthians 5:21
- More than conquerors - Romans 8:37
- Heavenly citizens - Philippians 3:20
- Heirs of God - Romans 8:17
- Forgiven - Ephesians 1:7
- Sanctified - I Corinthians 6:11
- Justified - Romans 5:1
- Redeemed - I Peter 1:18
- Eternally secure - John 10:28-29

Just knowing who we are in Christ gives us a sense of
security and conviction. If you haven't yet invited Christ
into your life, do it before you read another line. Pray
this prayer right now!

> *Lord Jesus, I believe You died for me on the cross, and*
> *rose again. I repent of my sin, and ask You to come*
> *into my life right now. I accept You as my personal*
> *Savior, and believe that You are the Christ, the Son of*
> *the living God! Amen.*

If you've never prayed that prayer, that's where it all starts!

KNOW HIM WHOM YOU HAVE BELIEVED

Our convictions are born out of our relationship with Christ. Being a Christian isn't a matter of only giving mental assent to a bunch of mechanical facts in the Bible. It is a commitment to a person, Jesus Christ. Paul wrote:

> *...I know whom I have believed, and I am convinced that he is able to guard what I have entrusted to him for that day (2 Timothy 1:12b).*

That's confidence. But you might be saying, "Well if I've accepted Christ as my Savior, don't I know Him?" Yes, but Paul said in Philippians (as a Christian) that he wanted to know Christ and the power of His resurrection (Philippians 3:10). It wasn't that he didn't know Christ, but the implication was that he wanted to know Him better and better.

KNOW WHAT YOU BELIEVE AND WHY

Every Christian bases his convictions on the revealed Word of God. We get our cue for living from holy scripture. It's the one sure thing that doesn't change. It's truths don't fluctuate, alter, or get revised every year. 2 Samuel 22:31 says that the Word of God is flawless. Proverbs 30:5 tells us that the Word of God is flawless. It's without error, that means you can rely on it, trust it, and know that its truths are enviable. Jesus said:

Heaven and earth will pass away, but my words will never pass away (Matthew 24:35).

Basing our convictions on God's Word means that we won't be passive, indifferent, or wishy-washy on subjects that deal with marriage, divorce, drunkenness, homosexuality, adultery, abortion, unmarried people living together, euthanasia, padding expense accounts, cheating on income taxes, etc.

BE COURAGEOUS IN THE FACE OF CRITICISM.

Never in my lifetime has the need been greater for men to rise up with a new courage. It's not enough simply to tolerate. I believe men need to go on the offensive and do great exploits for God. But in the midst of standing firm there will be great resistance, ridicule, and pressure. Paul's words in I Corinthians 16 need to be heeded:

Be on your guard; stand firm in the faith; BE MEN OF COURAGE, be strong (I Corinthians 16:13).

It's not a time to acquiesce, fold our hands, "go with the flow," live and let live, or wait and see. It's time to speak up and out, and stand on the eternal principles of God's holy Word. It will be neither popular nor pleasant at times, but it's what God has called us to do. Living a godly life and preaching godliness invites opposition and persecution.

In fact everyone who wants to live a godly life in Christ Jesus will be persecuted...(2 Timothy 3:12).

It comes with the turf. It's part of the package. It's normal combat. That's why Peter wrote:

Dear friends, do not be surprised at the painful trial you are suffering, as though something strange were happening to you (I Peter 4:12).

No, it isn't strange. It isn't out of the ordinary. People with Bible-based and godly convictions will be attacked in some way; either verbally, emotionally, or physically. You can expect it. That's why it takes godly courage to be men of conviction.

As I write these words, a battle is raging in the work place, especially on the West Coast, concerning what you can and what you can't say about your faith.

Though legislation is pending in many states, the message being delivered to all employees is not to mention religion on the job, at breaks, in the coffee room, or any place else. No religious jewelry is to be worn, no religious symbols are to appear on your desk, no religious music is to be played softly on the radio, no religious material may be made available, and no religious pictures are to appear on the wall. While the term "religious" is used, it's pretty well understood that what they're referring to is Christian, because of its evangelical nature. Not only is this move a suppression of free speech in America, it has stepped up harassment against Bible-believing Christians. No other group of people are really targeted.

The day is getting closer and closer when all Christians will have to make up their minds the way Peter and John did when they were told by authorities not to mention or teach anymore in the name of Jesus. Their response?

Judge for yourselves whether it is right in God's sight to obey you rather than God. For we cannot help speaking about what we have seen and heard (Acts 4:19b).

Men, especially, need that courage today. I believe there is a sifting in progress right now and God is sovereignly allowing many things to happen that will reveal who means business and who doesn't. Soon people won't be able to be "Mr. Looking-both-ways." One will have to express their convictions with boldness, fearlessness, and confidence, REGARDLESS of the consequences. It may eventually mean losing your friends, maybe losing your job, and maybe, ultimately your life. But convictions must be stood upon firmly.

SHARE CHRIST WITH OTHER MEN!

You may be saying, "I can't get into that witnessing stuff. I just freeze up when you start talking about that." Well, relax, I'm not talking about some formal theological explanation that can only be given by trained clergymen. I'm talking about your personal testimony of what Christ has done in your life so far. Peter said it best:

But in your hearts set apart Christ as Lord. Always be prepared to give an answer to everyone who asks you to give the reason for hope that you have. But do this with gentleness and respect... (I Peter 3:15).

Let's break that down!

"Always be ready..." That means watch for those golden opportunities that God gives you daily to put in a good word for Christ. You don't have to pray for the opportunities to come. They will. Just pray for wisdom to detect them when they do and for courage to speak. Sit on ready!

"...give the reason for your hope..." This is where it gets fun. If you're saved, you have reasons why you received Christ. Those reasons are: salvation, eternal life, abundant life, power, the presence of His Holy Spirit, fellowship, etc.

Your personal testimony needs to include three elements:

- *Before you accepted Christ (20 percent). Share with a man what your life was like before Christ came in.*
- *When you accepted Christ, how did it happen?*
- *Since you accepted Christ, what has it meant?*

Very simply put, tell them briefly what Christ means to you. I heard a business man recently share this:

"My life was a mess. My business was in shambles, my marriage was on the verge of breaking up, my kids were in trouble, and I was woefully overweight. A business associate asked me one day at lunch if I knew I would go to heaven when I died. I was stunned! I had never thought about it. He then shared with me how I could know for sure that I would end up in heaven, so I asked Christ into my heart. Since receiving Christ, I've learned Biblical financial principles and my business is prospering, my marriage is on good footing now, and my children have all invited Christ into their lives. Our whole family is different, thanks to Christ."

Reread that again and time it. According to my watch, even reading it slowly it takes only 40 seconds! But what a testimony and he's led many men to Christ by it.

A witness is someone who tells another what he has seen and heard. That's it. If Christ has made a difference in your life, talk about it to others. You'll be surprised at how interested they will be in what you have to say.

Some people say, "It doesn't make any difference what you believe, as long as you're sincere." If I sincerely believe I'm taking aspirin, but it's really strychnine, will my sincerity save me? If I sincerely believe that driving south in the northbound lane of the freeway is right, will my sincerity avoid a head on collision? Hardly. Sincerity is fine as long as it's based on facts and truth.

Our generation is slipping quickly today because people are abandoning their convictions. You may have the fastest race car in the industry, it may be painted with the best paint money can buy, but if the tires are cheap or old you'll lose the race...and maybe your life. Just as we need tires for a good foundation on the race track, so we need authentic convictions as our foundation in the race of life!

We have a tendency to think, "I'm just one man, can I make that much of a difference?" Could I remind you of something?

- In 1645 ONE vote gave Oliver Cromwell the control of England.

- In 1649 ONE vote caused Charles I of England to be executed.
- In 1776 ONE vote gave America the English language instead of German. Thomas Jefferson and John Q. Adams were elected president by one vote in the Electoral College.
- In 1845 ONE vote brought Texas into the Union, along with California, Oregon, and Washington!
- In 1868 ONE vote saved President Andrew Johnson from impeachment.
- In 1876 ONE vote gave Rutherford Hayes the presidency of the U.S. and that vote was cast by a congressman from Indiana, who himself won his own election by only ONE vote.
- In 1923 ONE vote gave Adolph Hitler leadership of the Nazi Party.
- In 1960 ONE vote per precinct elected John Kennedy president of the United States!
- One vote, one man, one conviction...it makes a difference. Are you making a difference for your God, your home, your country today? Check your tires.

4

THE POWER OF A CLEAN CARBURETOR

A Man and His Purity

We were ready to take a long trip in our car. Only a few days before we were to leave the car starting running rough. It sounded and felt as if it was missing. Yet on checking the spark plugs, they were properly gaped and showed little wear. The car seemed to lose power at times. So, finally, I took it to my mechanic. He called me later in the day to tell me what the culprit was, a dirty carburetor. In his words, "It only takes a couple of grains of dirt located in the wrong place to affect your entire car." I thought, "Hmmm, what's true of a car is true of a person, it only takes a small amount of moral impurity to wreck our whole life!" Because this was before the days of sealed carburetors, he took it apart, cleaned it thoroughly, adjusted the throttle back to where it was supposed to be, and it ran as smooth as glass.

Carburetors are private, you can't see inside of them very easily and on today's cars, you can't see in them at all. In the mechanic's words, "The power of your car really starts in the CARBURETOR, because that's where its fuel supply is carefully regulated." I had never thought about it that way. A man's life tends to disintegrate when his moral purity is compromised and soiled.

You can believe that every race car driver, whether he's driving in Daytona or Indianapolis, is going to have a clean carburetor! Debris, grime, and foreign substance can rob his car of power and cause him to not even qualify, or to lose the race.

Man is a moral creature. God has made him different from the animal. Yet it seems almost half of all letters sent to advice-oriented newspaper columnists are answering questions from women whose husbands have committed adultery. Far more men fall into the pit of sexual impurity than women. It's as though no man escapes the subtle temptation to ditch the biblical standard and yield to the flesh. There is good news though. We don't have to cave in. We don't have to yield. We don't have to fall, then regret it later. If this area of our live caves in, it tarnishes every other area.

WHAT A CLEAN CARBURETOR IS TO A CAR, PURITY IS TO A MAN. If our soul is dirty, our power will cease!

There is no area that presents more of a struggle for men than in the area of moral purity. A man's sexual appetite is ferocious! Like hunger pangs, it cries out to be satisfied, quenched, appeased. If a man is married and has a good relationship with his wife, she satisfies that mammoth drive in his life. Solomon even wrote:

...May you rejoice in the wife of your youth...may her breasts satisfy you always (Proverbs 5:18,19).

Happy indeed is the man who is sexually fulfilled by the love of his wife. But miserable is the man who has been involuntarily placed on a sex diet by his wife. Such diets of deprivation increase temptation, and can drive men to sexual immorality.

If you're single, and follow the Biblical standard of morality, you are living a life of celibacy, yet the sex drive is still there, strong, demanding, and at times very pulsating!

Resistance tends to weaken in either of the two above situations until the temptation is given in to. Pretty soon, a man has lost the power God intended him to have to get him through life victoriously.

Moral impurity among males is at an all time high today. There are some reasons.

Availability And Acceptance Of Pornography

A multi-billion dollar business, pornography in all forms has become easily accessible to men, and thus has become pervasive. The "stigma" has somewhat been re-moved, and that's all some men needed to hear.

Visibility And Persuasiveness Of Sex

No generation has experienced what we're experienc-ing today. Billions are spent yearly to large advertising firms to clothe products in a sex package. If you don't believe it, check out the Calvin Klein ads. On billboards, TV, radio, magazines, newspapers, on the back of busses, wherever you turn, sex is selling products. In addition, sex is talked about more freely than ever between opposite sexes, which inevitably leads to license.

TOLERANCE OF IMMORALITY

Our generation has, in a sense, "legitimized" what used to be off limits. A good example of this is men having affairs outside of their marriage. When detected, it's not a big deal, "So I flubbed up. Hey, everyone makes mistakes." Those were the words of a famous athlete when his wife discovered he was sleeping around. No one seems shocked anymore, and when some brave soul calls to task a sleazy lifestyle, he's "judgmental and trying impose his morality on others." What a change from the previous generation!

Jeremy was 29 years old when I met him. Very handsome, inordinately financially successful for his age. He had been married for five years. They had one child. His voice sounded distraught at the other end of the phone. It was Saturday morning and we agreed to meet at the coffee shop.

Jeremy unfolded a sordid story of three years of infidelity with two different women. He was ashen white with fear that his marriage would be over. He shared with me how he became involved at his office, when Angie would walk by his desk and lightly brush up against him. He responded by doing the same and, slowly but surely, one thing led to another until they were having lunch together, then on to her apartment for what they joked about being "dessert." But as he talked with me, he was full of shame, remorse, and fear. "I know my wife well, and she won't give me a second chance, I just know she won't." In about one hour we would both know. His wife Lorrie burst into tears and wept uncontrollably at this violation. He tried to hold her, but she pulled away. Three days later after brokenness, then anger, then numbness, Lorrie, finally said the words, "I forgive you this time."

Their marriage is intact today, but the first couple of years were stormy and both were tempted to throw in the towel more than once.

An act of immorality begins in the mind. It begins with sexual lust. The question is often asked, "Can this burning desire inside of me be controlled and overcome? Can it be harnessed? Is there any way to keep it from controlling my life and winning every time? The answer is YES!

Steps To Overcoming Burning Sexual Lust

Below I've listed a sequential step-by-step plan to overcome the demon of lust in your life.

1. Confess It As Sin

Don't try to rationalize it as something natural, or normal. Don't try to minimize it by saying, "Well everyone struggles with this so I guess it's all right."

God will never, never intervene with His power until you are honest enough to stand before Him and acknowledge your impure thoughts and cravings as sin.

> *For everything in the world–the CRAVINGS OF SINFUL MAN, the LUST of his eyes and the boasting of what he has and does comes–not from the Father, but from the world (I John 2:16).*

When David had committed adultery with Bathsheba, he went into deep remorse and wrote what today is Psalm 51. Part of that Psalm needs to be prayed by us when thoughts of lust enter our mind:

> *For I know my transgressions, and my sin is always before me. Against you, you only, have I sinned, and done what is evil in your sight (Psalm 51:3-4).*

If you're struggling with lustful thoughts in your life right now, lay this book down, get on you knees if you can, and cry out to God in confession that what you're thinking is wrong. Tell God it's "stinking thinking." That's the first step.

2. Confess It To A Trusted Brother

"Do I really need to do that, I'm so ashamed!" Yes, but the key is finding a TRUSTED brother, one who will not blab what he knows, one with whom you feel a bonding and closeness. If you cannot think of anyone, go talk to your pastor, he'll understand. James 5:16 admonishes us to "confess our sins to one another." I believe God wants us to do this for the sake of accountability. God wants you to have a man in your life that can encourage you and build you up.

"Therefore encourage one another and build each other up, just as in fact you are doing (I Thessalonians 5:11).

God has some man out there that needs to encourage you and hold your feet to the fire, a man who will dare to ask you the hard questions.

3. Control What Passes Through Your Eyes And Ears!

Job nailed it down for us in the Old Testament:

"I made a covenant with my eyes not to look lustfully at a girl" (Job 31:1).

We need to strike a contract with our eyes. Jesus said in Matthew chapter six that the eye is the lamp of the body. What we allow through this "eyegate" will help determine whether or not we will be sexually lustful. This means we need to train our eyes to get focused OFF a beautiful woman, an ad in a magazine, or a TV screen that shows sexually explicit scenes. When you read 2 Samuel 11:1ff, you discover that David went through a denigrating process that culminated in an act of adultery.

He LOOKED

He LUSTED

He LAID

He LIED

That, sir, is a deadly process. David looked at Bathsheba while she was bathing. He immediately lusted after her. Then he longed for her to the point of sending for her. He then lay with her for sexual intercourse. Then he lied in order to get her husband killed so he could have her.

Guess where it all started...with a LOOK. No one doubts that had David taken his eyes immediately off of Bathsheba, and sought his God, the adultery would have never happened.

Perhaps this is why Paul wrote the Thessalonians:

Avoid every kind of evil (I Thessalonians 5:22).

4. Recognize The Source Of Sexual Lust

It helps us to know where those thoughts come from. It's clear they're not from God. That leaves only one other source, Satan. Jesus spelled it out clearly for us:

For from within, out of men's HEARTS come evil thoughts, sexual immorality...(Mark 7:21).

Make no mistake about it, sexual lust comes from within. It may be fed from what we see and hear, but in reality it occurs when we fail to walk by the power of the Holy Spirit in us and opt to live by the flesh (sinful nature) inside of us.

When you were saved, you were taken out of the sinful nature, but the sinful nature was not taken out of you. It lies there, but is powerless over us, UNLESS we pander to it, dance to its tune, and obey its suggestions.

5. Know Where Lust Leads

James says there is a cycle to sin:

...but each one is tempted when, by his own evil desire, he is dragged away and enticed. Then, after

desire has conceived, it gives birth to sin; and sin when it is full grown gives birth to death (James 1:14-15).

Notice the cycle, and where it eventually leads;
- Temptation
- Sin
- Death

Lust left unchecked, unchallenged, unconfessed and unrepented of, will eventually take a person to spiritual death. Once you get in the loop (by saying yes to temptation) the slide becomes very fast, and the momentum allows for no turning around. As men, we need to nip it in the bud, and learn to say "NO" to temptation. It's easier to say NO up front, than to try to back out of the process later.

6. Know And Obey God's Sovereign Will

Lust and immorality are contrary to the will of God. We have that made very plain for us in Scripture.

It is GOD'S WILL that you should be sanctified: that you should avoid sexual immorality; that each of you should learn to control his own body in a way that is holy and honorable, not in passionate lust like the heathen, who do not know God...(I Thessalonians 4:3-5).

It can't be said any clearer! God's will is for us to be sanctified. The word means to be set apart as holy. We are already holy positionally, God has made us holy by the blood of Christ but God wants holiness in practice as well.

The Bible says that we were chosen before the creation of the world to be HOLY and BLAMELESS (Ephesians 1:4).

7. *Allow God's Word To Cleanse Your Mind Daily*

This is a powerful tool. This point really spells the difference whether we are going to be the victims in the area of lust or the victors. Getting into God's Word daily; reading it, meditating on it, memorizing it, and applying it.

Paul wrote these words:

You were taught, with regard to your former way of life, to put off your old self, which is being corrupted by its deceitful desires; to be made new in the attitude of your minds... (Ephesians 4:22-23)

How are we "made new in the attitude of our minds?" Only by sending our thoughts through the sieve of God's Word daily. Paul spoke of putting "on the new self, which is being renewed in knowledge in the image of its Creator." (Colossians 3:10)

It's that daily renewal from getting into God's Word that drives away, and keeps away, sexual lust. It works, try it. Let me suggest to you that you spend the next month reading John 15 every day (30 or 31 days) and tell God that you want that chapter to renew your mind. Try it.

8. *Serve The Lord With Gladness*

I have found that men who spend time serving the Lord in some kind of ministry on a consistent basis, rarely fall victim to uncontrollable sexual lust. It doesn't mean that they no longer battle the problem, but victory is more easily attained if they're found faithful in service.

9. *Develop A Deeper Intimacy With Your Wife*

You may be asking, "How do I do this?" I believe in being pragmatic, so here's a list.

Romance her with flowers, candy, jewelry, notes, little acts of kindness. In giving affection, it will boomerang and you will receive added affection!

Make her your best friend. Confide in her, take walks with her, spend more time with her than you're now spending.

Shower her with compliments, not just flattery. Affirm her, praise her for her special touch in the house or on a meal.

Let love-making begin long before she reaches the bedroom. It may be a compliment after dinner, an offer to help with the children, a hug, a touch, words of affection early in the evening.

Determine that she alone will be the object of all your lovemaking, and that all your affection will be showered on her exclusively.

An interview occurred many years ago between Dallas Cowboy quarterback, Roger Staubach, and Phyllis George. She shocked Roger by asking him, "How do you feel when you compare yourself with Joe Namath, who is so sexually active and has a different woman on his arm every time we see him?" In his usual cool way

Staubach responded, "I'm sure I'm just as sexually active as Joe. The difference is all of mine is with one woman." [1]

That was Staubach's greatest score of all. Did (does) Roger Staubach not have lustful thoughts at times? Of course he did and I'm sure does, but the difference is clear; he has learned to draw from the limitless power of the Holy Spirit inside of him for resources found no place else. We can too!

I'm thinking of a man by the name of Daniel. As a young man he maintained his purity steadfastly. He was a man of conviction and with resolute faith, he stood up to a pagan king with nothing more than the power and the promise of God. We have no record that he lied, cheated, indulged in sexual pleasures, or in any other way compromised. God used him in a great way, and his story is preserved in the book of Daniel in God's Word.

Here is a prayer I find myself praying over and over. I thought you might like to read it, and make it your prayer too.

Dear God, I'm a man...fearfully and wonderfully made. Save me from the foolishness of playing with fire. Let Your cooling waters be lavishly poured over the heat of my lust. Sanctify my thinking, crucify my wandering, electrify my love for You, and mortify my wrong desires! My only hope of victory lies in You and You alone. Lord Jesus, I stand today in Your power, by Your strength, for Your purpose, and on Your word. Cleanse me by Your blood, and redirect my thinking to desire nothing or no one but You. Amen.

5

THOSE RACING BUDDIES

A Man and His Friends

A man with racing in his blood finds 99 percent of his friends at the race track. His very close buddies are the maintenance men, the mechanics, his general team in the pit, and believe it or not, even the competing drivers. If he bonds at all as a man, it's mostly with these guys. They know, they understand, they talk the lingo, they sense the pressures. In short, they are able to empathize. High-fives and bear hugs are not out of order here. Usually there will be one or two guys from the crew with whom he bonds very closely. These are his racing buddies.

While we all admit that no man is an island, let's face it, most males are severely deficient in the friendship department. While our wives and daughters (and moms) develop a whole array of friends, most of us men have a very tough time bonding with other males. Oh, if you ask the average man how many friends he has, he'll tell you,

"Lots, too many to mention." What he usually means is that he's got guys at work he drinks coffee with, golfing and fishing buddies, guys he goes to games with, etc. But friends? Most men have very few if any. Why? There are some known reasons;

MEN ARE THINKERS, NOT FEELERS

Objective in nature, most men aren't naturally "drawn" to other guys emotionally like women. They think in terms of measurable goals, doable projects, and completion dates, but few think in terms of another human being with whom he can share his guts.

MEN ARE TASK-ORIENTED, NOT RELATIONAL

It's interesting to watch two women sit together on a plane. Within minutes they know one another's name, their children's names, how many grandchildren each has, and they exchange recipes. A man can sit next to another male on a plane and not exchange words for miles. He may never know the name of the man who is sitting one half inch from him! On the other hand, if they're comparing notes on a work project, you can't shut them up! Even then though the conversation will never get to a personal level on purpose.

MEN ARE COMPETITIVE IN SPIRIT

They want to win. Competitors usually have a passing acquaintance, but seldom a deep friendship. Usually a man's goal with another man is to beat him at tennis, racquet ball, in sales, or whatever.

MEN ARE NATURALLY SUSPICIOUS

While women, for the most part, are trusting creatures, men tend to question everything. If a mechanic quotes him a price on a water pump, he's thinking, "I wonder how much I'm being swindled for?" That suspicion tends to prevent any relationship from ever going further than "skin" deep.

MEN ARE NATURALLY NOT TALKERS

Since the development of a close friendship requires talking, fewer men establish close friendships. In a personal poll I conducted on an anonymous questionnaire, 243 out of 300 men said they could not name a best friend they were close to. Women are much more "social" people than men are. I think that part of this is due to the fact that there is a rugged individualism in most men. Most men won't just pick up the phone and call another man to see how he's doing. He may call to see how he's progressing on a project, or to find out how his kid did in Little League, but men, for the most part, are not talkers, but doers.

Men need friends, close friends, true friends, loyal friends, guys they can call at two o'clock in the morning and know they will listen. The pressure, stress and constant demand to perform and provide a living for their families, suggest to me that guys really need other guys with whom they can bond and relate.

The Bible mentions friendship more than we might think:

- Jonathan and David
- Ruth and Orpah
- Esther and Moredecai
- Paul and Timothy
- Mary and Martha, and Jesus

Solomon said it best many years ago:

As iron sharpens iron, so one man sharpens another (Proverbs 27:17).

One of the most beautiful sights in the Bible, in my opinion, is how Aaron and Hur held up Moses' arms when he was too weary to hold them up himself.

When Moses' hands grew tired, they took a stone and put it under him and he sat on it. Aaron and Hur held his hands up–one on one side, one on the other–so that his hands remained steady till sunset (Exodus 17:12).

Those are real friends, not just passing acquaintances. I think deep down, most men would love to have a close buddy; every Batman needs a Robin, every Huckleberry Finn needs a Tom Sawyer, every Butch Cassidy needs a Sundance Kid, every Amos needs an Andy. We really do need each other.

Here's a question, if you died, would your wife and kids have any problem finding six friends to carry your casket?

MOST MEN ARE OVER-SCHEDULED

Only in Ozzie and Harriet does the husband/father work a 40-hour week, have six hours of free time Monday through Friday evening, then have all day Saturday and Sunday free. Today, most men work a 50-plus hour week, have much more stress on the job than men in previous generations, and find themselves overscheduled, overextended, and lacking energy and initiative. There is little, or no, time to develop new friendships, or try to maintain old ones.

One man recently said to me, "Every week seems to get shorter and shorter, I have so little time to do anything." Can't we all relate to that? Yet it doesn't take away the fact that we really do need friends, men with whom we can share our deepest confidences, men with whom we can laugh, cry, or just sit in their presence. We need men in our lives bold enough to hold our feet to the fire, yet compassionate enough to literally hold us when we're falling apart.

Perhaps the male friendship of all friendships is the one between David and Jonathan in the Bible. David, you will recall, was being relentlessly pursued by Saul. Many attempts on his life had left David tired, confused, fearful, and frustrated. Saul's young son, Jonathan, was ordered by his father to kill David. He knew they were the best of friends, and that Jonathan would have no problem finding David. You don't have a problem knowing how deep the friendship was between David and Jonathan:

...but Jonathan was very fond of David...(I Samuel 19:1).

The word FOND is a very strong word in the original language. It means "affectionately taken." We're talking about a friendship that is as close as two men can be, in a nonsexual relationship. I believe that contained in David and Jonathan's friendship are all of the traits and characteristics of true friendship. We might call these:

THE MARKS OF GODLY MALE FRIENDSHIP

1.   *There is a close-knit relationship.*

> *After David had finished talking with Saul, Jonathan became one in spirit with David, and he loved him as himself (I Samuel 18:1).*

We're talking about a unity here that is unbreakable, a oneness that is akin to the oneness in marriage.

2.   *A reciprocal relationship, based on trust.*

Jonathan wasn't willing to just have another surface relationship with a man, David. He went deeper than that. He drew up a covenant:

> *And Jonathan made a covenant with David because he loved him as himself. Jonathan took off the robe he was wearing and gave it to David, along with his tunic, and even his sword, his bow, and his belt (I Samuel 18:3-4).*

Jonathan's gesture showed the depth of his love for David. He meant business in this friendship. The giving of all of Jonathan's military paraphernalia indicates a friendship built on explicit trust.

3. *A friendship that transcends familial relationships.*

Sometimes deep friendships are between blood kin, but most of the time they transcend blood relatives. Jonathan's commitment to David exceeded even his loyalty to his father.

> *Saul told his son Jonathan and all the attendants to kill David. But Jonathan was very fond of David, and warned him, "My father Saul is looking for a chance to kill you. Be on your guard tomorrow morning; go into hiding and stay there. I will go out and stand with my father in the field where you are. I'll speak to him about you, and will tell you what I find out"* (I Samuel 19:1-3).

Please notice something...Jonathan was willing to enter into conflict with his dad to defend his friend. A bond existed between David and Jonathan that went even deeper than the relationship between Jonathan and his father. Truth and integrity were at stake here, and Jonathan was not willing to sacrifice truth on the altar of blood relationship. When "push" came to "shove" Jonathan chose to side with his friend, because of what was right and true. There was a "shared value system" between Jonathan and David that didn't even exist between Jonathan and his own blood father. Their shared value system didn't have anything to do with their interests, occupation, personal likes and dislikes, but with what was right and honorable. Jonathan was a prince, David was a shepherd; they were not even from the same economic category, but they bonded on the basis of truth and honor. This is why friendship between males is more than playing golf, hunting, fishing, or going to a football game together.

Listen to these verses from I Samuel 20 concerning the loyalty and love between these two guys:

> *"But if my father is inclined to harm you, may the Lord deal with me, be it ever so severely, If I do not let you know and send you away safely. May the Lord be with you as he has been with my father. But show me unfailing kindness like that of the Lord as long as I live, so that I may not be killed, and do not ever cut off your kindness from my family–not even when the Lord has cut off every one of David's enemies from the face of the earth" (I Samuel 20:13-15).*

That's friendship that transcends closeness even to blood relatives!

4.   *True friends stand up for one another, even when it's not popular...even when it's more convenient, more economical, and more pleasant to jump ship.*

In the story of David and Jonathan, I'm moved by the fact that Jonathan stood up for his friend to his friend's arch enemy. Let these words of Jonathan to his father soak in:

> *Jonathan spoke well of David to Saul his father and said to him, "'Let not the king do wrong to his servant David; he has not wronged you, and what he has done has benefited you greatly. He took his life in his hands when he killed the Philistine. The Lord won a great victory for all Israel, and you saw it and were glad. Why then would you do wrong to an innocent man like David by killing him for no reason?"* (I Samuel 19:4-5).

Wow! What a speech! If we had a video recording of this I think we would see and hear a pathos in Jonathan's face and voice you just don't get on the printed page.

It was not the "in" thing for Jonathan to plead David's case. It was, in fact, risky. Jonathan risked his very future as King to plead the case of his friend, whom he was convinced had done no wrong. Are you willing to do that for another man? Am I?

A few years back, a man in our church was charged with sexual harassment on the job. The charge was completely unfounded. When he went before a hearing board that would determine whether or not he would keep his job, his friend, who sat two desks away, showed up unrequested, risking his job and his reputation. He gave a testimony about the credibility of his friend. The case was eventually dismissed, but the deciding factor was that testimony! Jonathan stood to lose much by standing up for David. He stood to lose even more by not doing it!

5. *A true friend holds nothing back from his buddy.*

I'm impressed with one verse of scripture in I Samuel 19:

So Jonathan called David and told him the whole conversation. He brought him to Saul, and David was with Saul as before (I Samuel 19:7).

He told David the WHOLE conversation, his and Saul's. He didn't try to hide the negative and only dwell on the positive. Total transparency is essential in friendship. That kind of honesty ends up bringing good. In this case, David was restored to Saul, even though it was temporary.

6. *A real friend can share his fears with his buddy.*

Look again at the openness David had with Jonathan. Only two verses later, jealousy overcame Saul again, and while David was playing his harp, Saul tried to pin him to the wall with a spear. David escaped that night realizing again that his life was in severe danger from this mad man. Through his wife's help, David had to escape from his own house, as Saul relentlessly hounded him. Discouraged, fearful, and running out of steam, David had to get to his best friend, Jonathan.

> *Then David fled from Naioth at Ramah and went to Jonathan and asked, "What have I done? What is my crime? How have I wronged your father, that he is trying to take my life?...Yet as surely as the Lord lives and as you live, there is only a step between me and death" (I Samuel 20:1,3b).*

You can feel the fear in those words. As men, we go through times of fear. Fear of not being an adequate provider, fear of failure, fear of not measuring up, fear of falling into temptation...fear abounds. We need a friend with whom we may share all of our fears. I remember going to lunch with a man who had no friends. At lunch he said, "I probably know you as well as I know any man, and I'm scared. For the past three months I have been sexually impotent. I fear I'm losing my manhood,

and I had to confide in someone, I need help." I was awed
that he trusted me enough to share a large fear in his life.
Fortunately, once we got to the root of the problem, which
was heavy stress from his job and a sick child, his impo-
tency was short-lived. I'll never forget seeing him in the
parking lot one day and he did a double "thumbs up." I
returned with a thumbs up and smiled. No one who saw
us knew what we were talking about, but we did, and a
friendship began that was healthy.

7. *A true friend puts himself at his friend's disposal.*

Notice what Jonathan says to David:

*"...Whatever you want me to do, I'll do for you" (I
Samuel 20:4).*

That's a friend! Jonathan was saying; "I'm at your
disposal, David. My time is your time, my money is your
money, my voice is your voice...you name it, I'll do it."

I have a friend whom I could call at any hour and he
would be ready to lay down his life for me. He once said,
"Bob, if it's not illegal, indecent, or immoral, I'll do it for
you." He meant what he said, and I know I can count on
him.

It's no wonder David said what he did to Jonathan:

*And Jonathan had David reaffirm his oath out of love
for him, because he loved him as he loved himself (I
Samuel 20:17).*

True friendship says "whatever the cost....count
me in."

8. *True friends don't hide their affection!*

Most men have a struggle in showing affection to other men. With the rising problem of homosexuality and its visibility, Christian men have become reluctant to demonstrate openly their love for their friends. But notice what David and Jonathan did:

> *...then they kissed each other and wept together–but David wept the most. Jonathan said to David, "Go in peace for we have sworn friendship with each other in the name of the Lord, saying 'The Lord is a witness between you and me, and between your descendants and my descendants forever.' " Then David left, and Jonathan went back to the town (I Samuel 20:41-42).*

Some of you are saying, "That's going a little too far, I'm not about to kiss my best buddy!" I hear you, but get the principle. When you're bonded to another man in deep friendship, all nonsexual touching is appropriate to the degree that both are comfortable. One of the beautiful things that Promise Keepers is bringing back among men is the big bear hugs that epitomize love and friendship.

9. *True friendship helps your buddy find strength in God.*

I suppose this is the deepest part of friendship between men. This statement, from I Samuel 23, says volumes:

> *And Saul's son Jonathan went to David at Horesh and helped him find strength in God (I Samuel 23:16).*

We do become "weary in well doing." We do become discouraged at times. We do lose heart. We do wonder at times how we're going to go on. How refreshing it is to have a friend.

I had such a friend who was a fellow pastor in another state. Through the years we developed a bonding that is hard to explain. Ed would call me long distance with regularity if I didn't think to call him first. We even found ourselves calling each other at the same time more than once. He seemed to call when I thought I could go no lower. His favorite question would be, "Bob, how's it really going? I couldn't fool him, he could read my voice. We got together as much as we could. There was no one I was closer to than Ed.

I once invited him to speak for me on a Sunday evening. The Saturday before we had driven together to a conference where I spoke, and the fellowship was sweet. We laughed together, cried together, dreamed together, prayed together, and hugged each other scores and scores of times. On the next day, Sunday, I got a call from the police that Ed had been in an auto accident at the motel where he and his wife were staying. I rushed over only to see the ambulance close its doors to whisk him off to the hospital. Two hours later, in the waiting area of the emergency room where my wife and I sat with his wife, the doctor came in to say, "I'm sorry, we did all we could, but your husband expired."

His wife lost a husband, and a good one. His only child lost his father. I lost a dear friend, and I wept for days. My first thought was; "Ed will never strengthen me again in the Lord, in this life." How I miss him to this day.

When Jonathan died, David gave his personal tribute in these very moving and strong words:

> *"I grieve for you, Jonathan my brother; you were very dear to me. Your love for me was wonderful, more wonderful than that of women" (2 Samuel 1:26).*

No, I don't understand the full import of that last phrase. Yes, I believe in their friendship was a love different from romantic love, but perhaps deeper than romantic love. One thing is for sure. Though it was a nonsexual, non-romantic love, it ran deep, and was much, much more than a casual acquaintance. We men need that kind of relationship with at least one man, and probably more.

Two little boys grew up in the same neighborhood in the Midwest, attended the same grade school, junior high school, and graduated on the same night from the same high school. They were close pals. One joined the service, and five days later, his grieving friend couldn't bear the loss, so he joined the service as well. They attended the same basic training, and oddly enough were both assigned to the same base on the West Coast. They found themselves in the same battalion, both going to Vietnam on the same day. They were both in the same offensive campaign.

One day when enemy fire was its worst, one of the young men noticed his buddy didn't come back in the evening. He requested his commanding officer to go and help him. The request was denied. The commanding officer said, "You will be killed, too, if you go out there looking for him." The young man defied his superior. He had to go. He spotted his friend lying facedown on the side of a ridge. As he got closer, he could see that his leg had been blown off, and he was bleeding profusely. Cradling his lifelong buddy in his arms and pulling him to his chest, he heard his friends last words, "I knew you would come..." Then he died. That's friendship.

In the race of life, we need friends. So, find a friend, make a friend, and be a friend. You'll survive the race much more fulfilled!

6

DRIVEN BY THE PURSE

A Man and His Money

I'll never forget finishing the tour of the Daytona race track. One woman in the van asked the tour guide, "What motivates these men to risk their lives, and invest so much time, money and effort to race?" His response was really no surprise to the rest in the tour group. "It's the purse, ma'am, it's the purse!" Oh, I'm sure a small part of the motivation is the mystique of racing. I'm sure the adventure of it is some of the motive. Certainly the excitement of the crowd and the flair of the sport both motivate. Make no mistake about it, the bottom line is to cross that finish line first for the purse, which today is hundreds of thousands of dollars.

Race car drivers are not the only ones "driven" by money. Most men have a real struggle in this area. In talking with hundreds of men across the country, I've found that whether a man earns $20,000 a year, or $250,000 a year, he will struggle with greed, selfishness, and lack of discipline when it comes to managing the resources God has given him.

I believe a passage of scripture in I John 2 was written primarily for men. It reveals that there are three broad areas in which most people struggle. I think men struggle in these areas more than women. It says:

> For everything in the world–the cravings of sinful man, the lust of his eyes, and the boasting of what he has and does–comes not from the Father, but from the world (I John 2:16).

Did you pick the three areas out?

"Cravings of sinful man"—SEX

"Lust of his eyes"—MONEY (THINGS)

"Boasting of what he has and does"—POWER

Those three pieces of dynamite must be handled very carefully by us men, or they will explode right in our face.

It's no secret that money issues are important issues in a majority of divorces in America. There are disagreements over how it is used, the lack of it, the misuse of it, the bondage of credit. The list is endless. Gentlemen, it's time to "Start Your Engines" in this department, and assume full leadership and responsibility.

Jerry "flagged" me down in the lobby of our church one day. "I've got to get with you soon, how about lunch?" Two whole weeks went by and we finally touched base. Jerry, a 38-year-old, owned a small but a very successful manufacturing company. From the outside one wouldn't have guessed, in a million years, that anything was wrong with his and Jane's marriage of ten years. They had two beautiful daughters, ages four and seven. They lived in an upscale neighborhood of fairly expensive homes. Over a bagel and salad, Jerry went straight to the matter. Because he had made a lot of money, his philosophy was that he should spend a lot of money. Jerry bought a summer cabin in the mountains, two snowmobiles, a fairly expensive pleasure boat, about $5,000 worth of new snow ski equipment, a small motor home, plus several other trinkets.

Jane felt he was out of control with spending. They were actually having a hard time servicing their debt. They were in complete disagreement over the way he was handling (or mishandling) money. The disagreement was so strong that she was considering a short separation for her to "sort out" her marriage. Jerry's words to me were, "Surely I have a right to do with my money what I want, after all I earn it." That's where we started.

What I shared with Jerry that day, and the two other times we met, is what I'll share with you. We might call this: "A Money Manifesto for a Godly Man." They are really principles of Biblical finance.

1. *First, Recognize That God is the Owner, and You are the Manager.*

We own nothing, God owns everything. Consider:

The earth is the Lord's, and everything in it, the world, and all who live in it...(Psalm 24:1).

"...for every animal of the forest is mine, and the cattle on a thousand hills. I know every bird in the mountains,

and the creatures of the field are mine. If I were hungry
I would not tell you, for the world is mine, and all that
is in it" (Psalm 50:10-12).

"The silver is mine and the gold is mine" declares the
Lord Almighty (Haggai 2:8).

If God is the owner, we are the managers. Our job is
to manage whatever He allocates to us. Matthew 25:14ff
gives a parable that Jesus told about this. He makes it
clear in the parable that the master (owner) entrusted to
the servants (managers) differing amounts of money. He
went on a journey, came back and demanded an account-
ing. The idea of the parable is clear. As a Christian, God
entrusts to us an amount of resources that differs with all
of us. He wants it managed well. He's concerned how we:

- Earn it
- Spend it
- Save it
- Give it

Part of "Starting Your Engines" and becoming men of
God is understanding this very first principle. Someday
God will ask everyone reading these lines, "What did you
do with what I entrusted to you to manage?" Gee? What
will we say?

2. Don't Make Money The Focus Of Your Life.

Money is not evil. It's good. Paul never said that money
was the root of all kinds of evil, but that the "love" of
money is (I Timothy 6:10). John Wesley said again and

again: "Gain all you can, save all you can, and give all you can."

Good advice, but money is "amoral." It's neither good nor bad. Its character is determined by how we use it (or abuse it). The Bible is clear, however, that while money is not evil, we're not to set our focus on it.

> *People who WANT to get rich fall into temptation and a trap and into many foolish and harmful desires that plunge men into ruin and destruction (I Timothy 6:9).*

The key word in that passage is WANT Some versions say DESIRE. In other words, it says, "Don't make money the focus of your life...don't attempt to become rich...don't put your hope in riches." Then is it wrong to make a lot of money? Not at all. Is it wrong to have a lot of money? No. If God wants to "bless the socks off of you," financially, good." But don't seek it, pursue it, and make it the number one goal of your life. And please remember what Jesus said:

> *How hard it is for the rich to enter the kingdom of God (Mark 10:23).*

No, he didn't say it was impossible, but it was hard. Why? Because Jesus knew that possessions would be a real problem area for most of us.

In the story of the rich young ruler, Jesus put his finger right on the man's problem: GREED and LOVE FOR MONEY. He came to Jesus with the right question, "What must I do to inherit eternal life?" He got the right answer.

*"Go, sell everything you have and give it to the poor,
and you will have treasure in heaven. Then come and
follow me."(Mark 10:21)*

Jesus put the man to the acid test. Though he asked
the right question of the right person, and got the right
answer, he did the wrong thing.

"He went away sad, because he had great wealth."
(Mark 10:22)

He wanted eternal life almost more than he wanted
anything else, but he wanted his money even more. How
sad. He made the mistake that many men make. They
spend the first half of their life amassing their wealth, and
the last half keeping others from getting to it. Both halves
are miserable! It doesn't have to be that way once we get
God's perspectives on money. So, while many can't handle
having a lot of money, it isn't wrong to have it if God
blesses you with it.

So, if God has blessed you with a gift for making a lot
of money, make it, by all means, PROVIDED...

1. You don't compromise your biblical convictions.
2. You don't neglect your family.
3. You don't become greedy with it.
4. You don't harm your health by doing it.
5. You don't let it consume your time so as to have
    none left for Christian service.
6. You're willing to be generous with it for Kingdom
    causes.

I cannot stress how absolutely necessary the above
conditions are. Wise Solomon said this:

Do not wear yourself out to get rich; have the wisdom to show restraint. Cast but a glance at riches, and they are gone, for they will surely sprout wings and fly off to the sky like an eagle (Proverbs 23:4-5).

Jesus said:

...a man's life does not consist in the abundance of his possessions (Luke 12:15).

Because men are driven by their ability to earn a livelihood, unfortunately, success has been measured by how much money a man is capable of earning. In our fallen state, men seem to think that if they don't make a lot of money, they're unsuccessful. If they do make a lot of money, they are successful. With God, success is not measured by how much we have, but who we are. Our sense of worth needs to be derived from who we are in Jesus Christ.

3. Begin A Program In Your Life To Get Out Of Debt.

Debt is not wrong. Nowhere in God's word is debt looked upon as sin. In fact, we find instruction in the New Testament commanding us to repay what we owe. Many people have used Romans 13:8 as a "proof text" not to borrow money. It simply says,

"Let no debt remain outstanding...." In other words, it's commanding us to pay our debts. So debt is allowed. If you back up to verse seven it says, "Give everyone what you owe him." That command presupposes it is all right to incur debt. What is wrong is to accumulate either an amount of debt that brings all of your life into bondage, or debt you cannot repay. Solomon stated another fact that is absolutely true:

> The rich rule over the poor, and the borrower is servant to the lender (Proverbs 22:7).

Debt brings us into a relationship with the lender that can be oppressive.

Debt at its best is living less that God intended us to live. God made a promise to the Jews, predicated upon their obedience to him.

> The Lord will open the heaven, the storehouse of his bounty, to send rain on your land in season and to bless all the work of your hands. You will lend money to many nations, but will borrow from none (Deuteronomy 28:12).

We've drifted far from the norm, I'd say.

Long-term debt is very much discouraged. Most people today don't blink at a 30-year mortgage on their home. It's interesting to me that in Scripture, seven years seemed to be the longest debt they had.

In debt, we need to avoid surety, or accepting a responsibility to pay without any way to make that payment. Finally, we need to avoid debt for depreciating items, like cars, refrigerators, boats, etc.

I believe if we men are going to "Start Our Engines" and regain the reins of true biblical leadership, we have to become responsible in the finance department. Debt-free living removes oppression. Debt-free living frees us from bondage. Debt-free living establishes a good testimony to others that we're men of God, who base all of our decisions on God's word, not on what's trendy.

2. Decide To At Least Tithe Of Your Income.

Of course, this means following the mandate of Malachi 3:10,11 that commands us to bring the whole tithe into God's storehouse. Jesus certainly endorsed tithing in Matthew 23:23, yet MOST Christian men are lax in this area of their life. I've found as a man, a husband, and the head of my household, that there are several reasons to tithe.

1. I'm commanded to do it.
2. It's fair.
3. It is a testimony to my wife and children about my priorities.
4. It honors and glorifies God.
5. It's a demonstration of my faith in God's ability to enable me to live off the nine-tenths I'm left to manage.
6. It keeps me from "stealing" from God what is rightfully His.

It prevents me from becoming self-serving and selfish.

While God calls for us as men to provide for our families, we are also warned about putting our hope in uncertain riches.

Command those who are rich in this present world not to be arrogant nor to put their hope in wealth, WHICH IS SO UNCERTAIN...(I Timothy 6:17).

It's a fine line we men walk in the finance department, yet I've found the following helpful. I call them THE TEN COMMANDMENTS FOR MEN AND THEIR FINANCE:

1   THOU SHALT KNOW THAT IT IS THE LORD WHO GIVES YOU THE POWER TO GET WEALTH.

2. THOU SHALT NOT MAKE MONEY THE FOCUS OF YOUR LIFE.

3. THOU SHALT NOT BORROW MONEY THOU CANST NOT PAY BACK!

4. THOU SHALT RESIST THE TEMPTATION TO EQUATE SUCCESS WITH HOW MUCH MONEY THOU HAST.

5. THOU SHALT TITHE OF THY INCOME AS A TESTIMONY THAT YOU TRUST GOD IN THIS LARGE AREA OF YOUR LIFE.

6. THOU SHALT LIVE WITHIN THY MEANS, EVEN IF IT MEANS LOWERING YOUR STANDARD OF LIVING.

7. THOU SHALT SEEK TO LIVE BY A BUDGET.

8. THOU SHALT UNDERSTAND THAT GOD WILL HOLD YOU ACCOUNTABLE WITH WHAT YOU DO WITH WHAT YOU HAVE.

9. THOU SHALT MAINTAIN UTMOST HONESTY IN EARNING THY INCOME.

10. THOU SHALT NOT BE A SCROOGE WITH
    THY FAMILY!

I truly believe that if we live by those financial commandments, God will greatly honor our leadership in this very important area of our life.

A poet said it well:

"Dug From The Mountainside, Washed In The Glen, Servant Am I, Or Master Of Men; Steal Me, I Curse You; Earn Me, I Bless You, Grasp Me, Hoard Me, A Fiend Shall Possess You. Lie For Me, Die For Me, Covet Me, Take Me, Angel Or Devil...I Am What You Make Of Me." [2]

7

YOUR
BIGGEST FAN

A Man and His Wife

The tour guide at Daytona was driving past the largest grandstand I had ever seen. "On race day, over 90,000 people are jammed into those stands, not counting the people in the middle of the track. But..." he went on to say, "there are only a few die-hard fans here today...they are the wives of the racers!"

I thought about that. What kind of women are the wives of the racers? In some cases, probably some of them are women who really wished that their husbands had another profession. I'm sure they all like the purse, but maybe not the process. Be that as it may, you can believe these gals are the true, blue fans...whether their husbands come in first, second, third or last....as long as they come in alive at the finish line.

We have a national crisis in our country. It manifests itself in crime, teen pregnancy, out of control drugs, and single parent homes, among other things. Our country is

89

in the shape it's in because our homes are in the shape they're in. Our homes are in the shape they're in, because marriages are in the shape they're in. Marriages are in the shape they're in because in many cases, the husband has abrogated his God-given responsibility to be head, the leader, the covering, and the provider for his wife and family. A very large percentage of men in this country have simply copped-out, acquiesced and abandoned their role. They're gone. A headless marriage and home is like a headless chicken, it runs aimlessly, then drops.

God has called you, the male, to be the Chief Executive Officer of your marriage and home.

> For the husband is the head of the wife as Christ is the head of the church...(Ephesians 5:23).

What does "headship" entail? It entails something that many men have never seen in their own homes when they were growing up. Like produces like. It's like one young, 28-year-old man, recently told me, "I don't know what it means to be the head of my marriage...I've never seen it in action." He was sadly confessing that his own father "checked in his credentials as the head of his home" long ago.

Men, if your wife is your biggest fan, and she is, what kind of person does that make you want to be? It ought to make you the kind of guy that is worthy of her devotion and admiration.

God's earliest description of a man is one of authority, a take-charge attitude, a leader:

Let us make man in our image, in our likeness, and let them rule over the fish of the sea and the birds of the air, over the livestock, and over all the earth, and over the creatures that move along the ground (Genesis 1:26).

We were created to take the initiative, to lead, to plow ahead, to pioneer. This does not mean dictatorship, but benevolent leading.

In fact, the Bible is clear about our role in marriage. We have only one, but it is multifaceted! We are called to love our wives as Christ loved the church.

Husbands, love your wives, just as Christ loved the church...(Ephesians 5:25).

That's a tall order. If Paul had just not put in the little phrase, "as Christ loved the church," it might have been a piece of cake obeying that command. If I'm to love my wife in that way, I've got to ask myself the question, "How did Christ love the church?" The answer is a little scary, but it is possible!

As we explore that passage in Ephesians, we see the plan.

LOVE YOUR WIFE WITH A PURIFYING LOVE

...to make her holy, cleansing her...(Ephesians 5:26).

I recently had a water purifying system demonstrated to me for my home. I was shown the secret to the whole thing. Tap water is forced through a filter which changes the water from hard to soft, from impure to pure. In a sense, husbands were designed by God to be filters that purify. I fully realize that a Christian wife is made pure positionally and practically by the blood of Jesus, but there is a sense in which her husband's role is to make her pure and protect her purity by his life. How does this happen?

First of all, it happens by keeping yourself pure–by keeping things like sexual lust, and the temptation to sin under strict control by the power of the Holy Spirit. Many husbands today are into X-rated movies and other forms of pornography. I once read where it's estimated that over 30 percent of American men are into some kind of fantasy or pornography on a regular basis. Stop it before it's too late!

It also means that you have a responsibility to protect your wife from all of the impurity that is floating around. This means you may have to take the initiative about what is read, what books and magazines are allowed into the home, and what is viewed by your wife on television. Ninety percent of all of the "soaps" on TV today have one sex scene after another. Turn it off...for you and for her.

A BEAUTIFYING LOVE

Please notice what verse 27 of Ephesians 5 says:

...to present her to himself as a radiant church, without stain or wrinkle or any other blemish (Ephesians 5:27).

I had a man say to me after 20 years of marriage, "My wife isn't beautiful anymore." My response was, "She's only the extension of what you have made her." You see, that man had not been in the business of beautifying her through the years. He had virtually caused every wrinkle that appeared on her face.

How does a man "beautify" his wife? Mainly by making sure she doesn't have to worry about your covering, your support, your respect, your provisions, your sexual intimacy, your attention. Many, many women worry about their husbands; about their habits, addictions, reckless life, or lack of discipline. You can love your wife with a beautifying love by allowing her to live a worry-free life, as far as you are concerned. This also includes holding her often, and verbally letting her know that apart from Jesus Christ, she is the most priceless gift God has given you.

A Nourishing Love

Part of loving your wife like Christ loves the church is to provide proper nourishment for her. Paul says:

> After all, no one ever hated his own body, but he feeds and cares for it, just as Christ does the church (Ephesians 5:29).

I was sharing this principle at a conference in the Midwest. To get the men's attention, I asked, "Are you feeding your wife?" Before thinking, a man blurted out, "Have you seen her lately?" He obviously missed my point, I wasn't talking about physical food, but spiritual food.

But you're already asking, "How is this done? Does this mean I'm to come home, sit her in a chair, open my Bible every night and say, 'Okay, it's time for me to teach you the word of God?'" Hardly!

You do, however, need to take spiritual headship in the following ways.

1) Share with her what you're getting out of your daily quiet time. (If you're not having a quiet time, this is difficult!)

2) Ask her to hear your memory work for the day or the week. (Of course, if you're not memorizing scripture, you'll draw a blank)

3) Share with her how your prayer life is doing. (That's right, if you're not having a prayer life, that's pretty hard to do.)

4) Share with her some insights about a Christian book you are currently reading. (Of course...you get the point!)

5). Take the initiative to pray with her daily, and let her know you're praying for her daily.

6) Take the initiative for encouraging her to go to special Christian seminars, concerts or services.

7) Take the initiative in ministering spiritually to your children, this will feed her in an indirect way.

Remember, your wife's Bible study leader, pastor, or father are not the primary spiritual care-giver. You are.

A CARING LOVE

Paul also said in verse 29 of Ephesians 5 that you are to "care" for your wife. This means letting her know where she stands in your scale of priorities.

A man and his wife were coming home in their car. As they pulled into the driveway, the next door neighbor was on his porch, at the door with a bouquet of flowers in one hand, a box of chocolates in the other, hugging and kissing his wife. The wife in the car said, "Look, Henry, YOU ought to do that!" His response? "But I hardly know the woman." I think he missed it.

We men need to know that there is one thing a woman can't survive long without. No, it isn't sex, it isn't money, not even a nice house...it's not knowing where she stands in your value system. If we're going to "Start Our Engines" in our marriage, our priorities will look like this:

Christ first
Wife and family second
Job third
Hobby fourth

A UNITING LOVE

For this reason a man will leave his father and mother and be united to his wife, and the two will become one flesh (Ephesians 5:31).

Leaving and cleaving—that's your assignment! Does that mean you as a man have to lose all individuality? Not at all. It does mean, however, that she knows you have blended into your life, her feelings, her needs, her emotions, and her reactions. It means you have lost your right to think of putting your needs first, it's now her needs first. How is this carried out practically?

It starts with an attitude of concern about her. It starts with saying, "Honey, how did your day go today? How did you sleep last night? How was your workout today at the club?"

While most couples who marry are opposites in many areas, there is a unity that makes them one.

Do you love your wife with this kind of love? As Christ loved the church? Of course, none of us men measure up to it completely, but that is God's standard that He has set for us.

What kind of husband are you being to your wife? Here's a list of "kinds" of husbands, maybe you ought to check the one you are.

The ABSENT husband.

The COMPLAINING husband

The CRITICAL husband

The INDIFFERENT husband

The PASSIVE husband

The CONTROLLING husband

The DECEPTIVE husband

The NON-COMMUNICATING husband

The ANGRY husband

The JEALOUS husband

The WORKAHOLIC husband

The TIGHT-FISTED husband

The ARGUMENTATIVE husband

The IMPATIENT husband

The VERBALLY-ABUSIVE husband

The PHYSICALLY-ABUSIVE husband

The PERFECTIONIST husband
OR...
THE HUSBAND WHO SEEKS TO LOVE HIS WIFE
LIKE CHRIST LOVED THE CHURCH.

I have found it very helpful to review a list of questions which I've had in my file for many years. I was told early in my own marriage by an older man to do an annual "full-scale investigation" of my own life in relationship to my wife by asking myself these questions. As you read them, let them be YOUR questions, and see how you fare.

_____ 1. Do I pray for my wife at least once a day?

_____ 2. Do I kiss my wife good-bye when I leave from work and kiss her again when I return from work?

_____ 3. Do I hug my wife at least once a day?

_____ 4. Do I compliment my wife consistently?

_____ 5. Am I quick to forgive my wife and keep short accounts when I feel she's offended me?

_____ 6. Am I careful to never let the "sun go down" on my anger?

_____ 7. Do I offer to help my wife with her job as homemaker and mother?

_____ 8. Am I careful to keep no secrets from my wife?

_____ 9. Do I call my wife from work (if allowed) to see how she's doing daily?

_____ 10. Do I say, "I love you" often to my wife?

Well, how did you fare? We men are so function and goal oriented, it's very easy for us to forget to show tenderness toward our spouse.

Gentlemen, "Start Your Engines." Your biggest fan is watching. She's your wife.

Mazie V. Caruthers wrote this. I think it's worth passing on to the rest of you husbands. It's titled, "The Prayer of Any Husband."

> *Lord, may there be no moment in her life*
> *When she regrets that she became my wife,*
> *And keep her dear eyes just a trifle blind*
> *To my defects, and to my failings kind!*
> *Help me to do the uttermost that I can*
> *To prove myself her measure of a man,*
> *But if I often fail as mortals may,*
> *Grant that she never sees my feet of clay!*
>
> *And let her make allowance, now and then,*
> *That we are only grown-up boys, we men,*
> *So, loving all our children, she will see,*
> *Sometimes, a remnant of the child in me!*
>
> *Since years must bring to all their load of care,*
> *Let us together every burden bear,*
> *And when death beckons one its path along,*
> *May not the two of us be parted long.* [3]

A good prayer! Remember guys, when you're racing through life to do your best to win at the end, and thousands are cheering you on, just remember there's really only one cheer that counts in those stands. It is the cheer of the lady to whom you once said:

"To love and to cherish, till death do us part."

8

RACING BY
THE RULES

A Man and His Integrity

I had never met Jared until he showed up one day un-announced to see me. He was tall, tanned, trim, with coal black hair. Although only in his mid-thirties, he looked to me like a paragon of success. He got right to the point, fast. "Pastor, I can't go on with my life one day longer the way I am. I'm a pathological liar, and the lies have caught up with me. I stand to lose my business, my wife, the respect of my children, and I have ulcers that are destroying the walls of my stomach. I need help." That was for "openers."

As Jared's story unfolded, I discovered his lies began when he was in the sixth grade when he told the other boys that his father was a famous major league ball player. He shared how he had to continue with other lies to cover that lie up as his friends would see his plumber father drive his truck home at night. As a teenager, his lies became more severe as he lied about his age in order to buy beer, cheated on tests to get out of high school, and told a series of lies to get into college. The lies continued until he was thrown out of college. He met a woman to whom he lied about his life, and they were married. He was into his marriage only six months when a string of affairs began and continued. When he tested positive for syphilis, he lied to his wife saying he had a bad yeast infection that he had contracted from the club where he worked out. Jared ran an auto-repair shop, and was caught several times charging for work not done.

Now it was all caving in. His integrity was nonexistent, and his conscience could no longer carry the load. Fortunately, after three or four more sessions, in which we did an in-depth Bible study, Jared was freed from his lying spirit. Today he calls himself a "new man."

Every car racer knows that you race according to the rules, or you pay the piper at the end. Race tracks around the country are strewn with the wreckage of men who tried to bend the rules, circumvent the rules, or ignore the rules. Many are the men who were disqualified for having illegally-modified engines, non-regulation tires, or supplemented fuel in their tanks. The fines and the shame become too high a price to pay for the luxury of coloring outside the lines.

The average Christian man today is constantly challenged to "bend the rules" in business, in pleasure, in his personal life, in marriage, and in family. The pressure is great to live beneath a life of solid integrity.

Living "above reproach" in today's world is hard to do. Being honest and transparent is hard to do. There are many subtle things we do that we would never call dishonest, yet they undermine integrity.

You give the clerk a five-dollar bill for a $1.98 item, and she gives you the change for a twenty. Do you keep it and walk out?

You make a personal long-distance call at work, but charge it off to business. Is that right?

You take home a stapler from the office, because you need one at home, and requisition a new one at work. Right or wrong?

In order to get the contract, you fudge a bit about the quality of the product. What about it?

A salesman calls on the phone, you step into the hallway for a moment so your secretary can say, "I'm sorry he just stepped out of his office." Is that accurate and honest?

You lose fifty dollars in a dice game, and opt not to tell your wife. Is that lying?

Your boss issues an edict to all sales people to not divulge the defects in their product. Do you comply or say no?

Lack of integrity in the business world is nothing new. In the eighth century B.C. Amos cried out against the dishonest practices of his own day:

> ...*skimping the measure, boosting the price and cheating with dishonest scales, buying the poor with silver and the needy for a pair of sandals, selling even the sweepings with the wheat (Amos 8:5b-6).*

Part of the Mosaic law dealt harshly with dishonesty in business practices.

> *Do not have two differing weights in your bag,–one heavy, one light. Do not have two differing measures in your house–one large, one small. You must have accurate and honest weights and measures, so that you may live long in the land the Lord your God is giving you. For the Lord your God detests anyone who does these things, anyone who deals dishonestly (Deuteronomy 25:13-16).*

Solomon, the wealthiest man that ever lived, said it well:

> *The Lord abhors dishonest scales, but accurate weights are his delight (Proverbs 11:1).*

God made it clear to Israel, in Leviticus 19:35-36, that they were to use an honest ephah (a dry measurement) and an honest hin (a liquid measure). High-balling, price-fixing, expense-padding, bid-rigging, call it what you will, it's dishonest. Lying takes on many forms. Here are a few:

WITHHOLDING ALL OF THE TRUTH

A friend of mine went back to the man who sold him a car whose transmission was shot. The man said to him, "I didn't lie to you, I just didn't tell you everything I knew about the car." Is that lying? Yes, because it's creating an impression that is deliberately inaccurate. Paul reminded us:

> *Do not lie to each other since you have taken off the old self with its practices...(Colossians 3:9-10).*

EXAGGERATIONS

Some people lose their integrity when they exaggerate things, and embellish them. One woman recently told me how embarrassed she is when her husband tells company a story that he virtually makes up, but presents as true. Solomon spoke to this in Proverbs:

> *The sluggard says, "There is a lion outside!" or "I will be murdered in the streets!" (Proverbs 22:13).*

Most people exaggerate to make sure others are impressed, or because they don't think others will believe them. Men, make sure when you communicate with others, especially your wife, that you relate facts as they are, without embellishment.

LYING BY SILENCE

When we know something is true and can tell others it's true, but remain silent, it's a form of lying. Not long ago, a manufacturing company in Ohio sold the government fifty thousand pairs of simple pliers at $62 per pair! The government didn't catch it or question it in their trail of paperwork. The pliers could have been purchased in any hardware store, for about $1.19 each. When the company was nailed with price-gouging, its owners responded, "We opted not to say anything as long as they were willing to pay." (One wonders the mentality of those who do the purchasing for our government.) Another way we lie by silence and then justify it is by saying, "If I told my

wife I was frustrated about sex, she would think I was a
pervert..." or "If I told my boss about the way I feel he
would blow up..."or "If I told my family what a financial
mess we are in they would panic."

In the fifth chapter of Acts, Ananias and Sapphira
found out the hard way that God doesn't honor silence
when it's covering a lie. They sold a piece of property for
so much. They brought what was ostensibly the proceeds
of the sale and laid it at the apostles' feet. They didn't tell
an untruth, but their silence was meant to make the
apostles believe that what they had given was the whole
price of the land, and it wasn't. They had kept some back.
When they were nailed by Peter who told them that they
had lied to the Holy Spirit, Ananias fell dead! Three hours
later, his wife died too. God takes lying very seriously.

Scripture is very clear when it comes to integrity and
truth telling. To lie is to honor Satan, since he is "the
father of lies" (John 8:44). Lying guarantees consequences
we don't want to face. Solomon said it well:

> A false witness will not go unpunished, and he who pours
> out lies will not go free (Proverbs 19:5).

Paul put it even more clearly in reminding us that we
are all a part of each other:

> Therefore each of you must put off falsehood and speak
> the truth to his neighbor, for we are all members of one
> body (Ephesians 4:25).

When we misrepresent the truth, or exaggerate the
truth, or cover up the truth, we aren't just damaging ourselves, we're hurting others as well.

In this "race" we call life, we need to relate with others with a sense of honesty and integrity. I remember my first job at age 13. I was hired as a soda jerk in a drug store. Just over the ice cream box the owner had placed a large red sign that read, HONESTY PAYS! He was hoping it would keep employees like me from giving people more ice cream than they should have for their money.

The late Edgar A. Guest perhaps said it best:

I have to live with myself, and so,
I want to be fit for myself to know,
I want to be able as days go by,
Always to look myself straight in the eye;
I don't want to stand with the setting sun,
And hate myself for the things I've done.

I don't want to keep on a closet shelf,
A lot of secrets about myself,
And fool myself as I come and go,
Into thinking that nobody else will know
The kind of man that I really am;
I don't want to dress myself up in a sham.

I want to go out with my head erect,
I want to deserve all men's respect;
But here in the struggle of fame and pelf,
I want to be able to like myself.
I don't want to look at myself and know
That I'm bluster and bluff and empty show.

I never can hide myself from me;
I see what others may never see;
I know what others may never know;
I never can fool myself and so,
Whatever happens I want to be
Self-respecting and conscience free. [4]

I find myself with the same wish that great poet had. What about you? I think a good life-verse for every man is this:

> *In your teaching show integrity, seriousness and soundness of speech that cannot be condemned, so that those who oppose you may be ashamed because they have nothing bad to say about us (Titus 2:7b-8).*

9

THE INDOMITABLE PASSION

A Man and His Witness

Several years ago I was conducting a Church-Growth Conference in Florida. Part of the conference was going out, into homes, and sharing the gospel with people. A layman in the church and I drove to our assigned address. The first thing I noticed as we walked up on the porch was the insignia into which the doorbell button had been placed. It was in the shape of a race car. We pushed the button, and a young man answered the door with a T-shirt which read, "Happiness is racing!"

In the living room, about a dozen trophies dominated the shelves, you guessed it, in the shape of race cars. To top it all off the television was tuned to the time trials at Talladega. We didn't have to be rocket scientists to figure out that this guy was very much into racing. We asked the obvious question, "Are you a race car driver?" We weren't quite ready for the response, "Am I a race car driver? What else would anyone be?" He then began rattling off statistics,

names, records broken, and fatalities. He pulled out
scrapbook after scrapbook of races he had won in the
minor leagues of race car driving. His face lit up as he
rattled off all of the information...it didn't take us long to
know what the passion of his life was. In his words, "Once
racing gets into your blood, it's there for life!"

If the men of America are going to "Start Their
Engines" and be serious about the race of life, we need to
check our passion. What winds our clock as Christian
men? What turns us on? What lights our fire and rings
our bell?

When we left that race-car driver's house that night, I
asked myself, "What would happen if every Christian man
in America became as passionate and compelled about
winning other men to Christ as that young man was about
telling us the racing story?" Wow! A mammoth spiritual
revolution would occur that would shake our country to
the core.

Women do a much better job of sharing Jesus Christ
with other women, than men do sharing with other men.
Why? They are much more relational, and have an easier
job of releasing their passion.

Most Christian men I've met will do about anything.
They will help paint the church building, usher, teach a
class, drive a bus, serve on a committee, plus a myriad of
other things. It's great to see men give of themselves. But
when it comes to talking to other men about their
relationship with Christ, many guys freeze up. Paul had
no problem admitting the passion of his life:

*"...I consider my life worth nothing to me, if only I may
finish the race and complete the task the Lord Jesus has
given me–the task of testifying to the gospel of God's
grace (Acts 20:24).*

Paul ate, slept, prayed, lived, and longed for one
thing—the winning of others to Jesus Christ. No doubt,
that was his passion. He even said that he was willing to
become all things to all men so that by all means he may
save some (I Corinthians 9:22). You can almost feel his
passion bleed through.

We once had a man in our church, who at his own
expense, would have tracts printed. He would then stand
on the busiest street corner of Seattle, all day, once a week,
and try to talk to men about Christ. In his words, "I wake
up thinking about the lost, and I go to bed thinking about
the lost...their hopeless faces won't fade from my mind."
Here was a man with a passion, and he attempted to ful-
fill that passion in a rather unorthodox way. But at least
he was doing something.

What will it really take for us to become "men-
affectors" for Christ?

See Other Men Through The Eyes Of Christ

What do I mean? When men see other men, they think
of all kinds of things. "There's a guy that might be a pros-
pect for my product," or "There's a guy that might get me
a job," or "There's a guy I bet I can beat at tennis," or
"There's a guy that can make connections for me." The

list goes on. We need to learn to see men through the eyes of Jesus, who looked at them with compassion. I'm doing my best to see men with the thought, "Do they know Christ?" I'm praying that God will make me cognizant of where men are in their spiritual lives.

1. *Know Whom and What you Believe In and Develop Your Own Testimony.*

Obviously, that's where it starts. I once sat at a meeting of the Christian Business Men's Committee and heard an attorney say, "We're either missionaries or a mission field." He was right. One of the finest testimonies I've ever heard was from a semi-literate warehouse worker. He said, "I don't know the Bible all that well, but I do know this. I used to be mean, selfish, and violent. One day I invited Christ into my life, and He changed me so thoroughly, my old friends could not recognize me. I'm not what I'm going to be, but thank God, I'm not what I used to be." Then he sat down, and in that meeting I saw 12 men come to Christ. The testimony of a changed life and a satisfied "customer" is not something that can be manufactured. That very simple man said to me after the meeting that night that he knew the Bible was God's Word, that sin was real, that Jesus was the Savior, that hell awaits the wicked, and heaven awaits the saved, and that he knew he was going to heaven because of what Jesus did for him when he died on the cross. Here's a man who may have only completed the sixth grade, but he had no problem sharing his testimony.

In the hills of West Virginia, a coal miner, who was a drunk and violent husband, went to a meeting and got saved. The next day, his fellow employees had heard about it and began to tease and taunt him about what he had done. They said, "You really don't believe those Bible stories about Jesus turning water into wine, do you?" His response was golden. "I don't know whether Jesus turned water into wine, but I know he turned beer into furniture and groceries for me when he saved me."

When was the last time you shared your testimony with another man? It doesn't have to be as dramatic as the two above, it may be a simple testimony that you had the privilege of growing up in a Christian home, and came to Christ as a little boy. That's a valid and effective testimony. It doesn't matter what your testimony is as to how you came to Christ, but are you sharing it with other men?

2. Develop Friendships With Other Non-Christian Men So That Lifestyle Evangelism Can Take Place.

I love the way Dr. Joe Aldrich puts it when he speaks on this topic. He says that we men must play the music before we add the lyrics. By "playing the music" he means developing relationships first, winning other men's friendships and confidence before we start spilling our passion out to them.

I know men who play racquetball only with non-Christian men, just so they can show them that Christian men aren't a bunch of pansies! Soon the opportunity comes to add the words (the gospel), but when you do, it's very

authentic, and not "canned." Most men are not so interested in all the theological intricacies of the gospel, and its
mystique, as much as, "Does it work?" One man's recent
testimony at our church was short, but very powerful. He
said before he accepted Christ, his life was full of stress
because of his job and his family situation. After he accepted Christ, the same stress was still there, but through
the power of Christ and the promises of God's Word, he
was able to handle that stress and channel it for good.
When he said that, I could tell he had the attention of a lot
of men in our audience.

3. Tell the Gospel Clearly and Simply.

I've found that if we keep things in a testimonial context we come across most believable. Here's an example.

"Bill, I discovered that I really needed what God was
offering because I found out something about myself I
didn't know before. I found out that I, and the whole human race, have a disease called sin. We're born with it. I
further found out that no man has the ability to rid his life
of this fatal disease, which has separated us from God.
But what I couldn't do, God did do, coming in the person
of Jesus Christ to become the serum for my disease. Jesus
died on the cross, and God accepted his poured out blood
as full payment for my sins. He was buried and, on the
third day, was raised from the dead. I found out from the
Bible that what He died to give me I could receive by believing in Christ, repenting of my sins, and openly confessing the name of Christ. Well, I did that, and a miracle

happened....I was saved. Bill, would you be willing to invite Jesus into your life right now?"

I timed the above message. It took me 47 seconds! What did it cover?

The NEED for salvation, our sin. Romans 3:23 says, "All have sinned."

The INABILITY of man to do anything about his sin problem. Jeremiah 2:22 says: "Although you wash yourself with soda and use an abundance of soap, the stain of your guilt is still before me..."

The PROVISION of God...Jesus Christ. He is God's answer to our sin. John 3:16 would come in handy here.

The WAY we receive it...by faith. "Believe in the Lord Jesus, and you will be saved."

It's not complex, not difficult, not unclear, not irrational. It's the old, old story that millions have heard and acted upon. "But..." you're saying, "...what if they're turned off by it, or say no?" Please remember, your work is done. It's the Holy Spirit's job to convict and convince (John 16:8), but it's your job to tell. I learned something long ago, GOD DOESN'T HOLD ME RESPONSIBLE TO BE SUCCESSFUL IN THE GOSPEL, BUT TO BE FAITHFUL! God has not called any of you to pound the Bible over the heads of your friends. He has called you to share with them the unsearchable riches of Christ. The late Daniel T. Niles gave the best definition of evangelism I ever heard. "Evangelism is one poor beggar telling another poor beggar where he can find bread."

Years ago I wrote a little tract that is used wide-spread, to this day. It presents the gospel like this:

- GOD MADE THE FIRST MOVE - He created man in His image, and desired fellowship and harmony.
- MAN MADE THE SECOND MOVE - He sinned against God, lost his position as righteous, was removed from the Garden of Eden. Since like produces like, every person born since Adam is, like Adam, sinful in nature.
- GOD MADE THE THIRD MOVE - He provided a remedy for man's sin so he could be restored to a position of righteousness once again. He did this by sending His only son into the world to be a sacrifice for sin.
- NOW IT'S YOUR MOVE! God is waiting for you to officially accept His remedy and solution to your sin problem. Believe on the Lord Jesus, and you will be saved.

I'm glad that God made the gospel a simple plan, because no one can say that they don't understand it.

4. *Pray For God To Give You Divine Appointments.*

I have an appointment book filled with man-made appointments each week. But more exciting is to pray daily, "Lord, you arrange my path to cross with another man who needs to hear my testimony." Guess what? God will answer that prayer, because evangelism is a front-burner issue with God.

5. *Understand That In Most Cases, Men Want To Hear What You Have To Say.*

The breakdown of our culture, at every level, has left men insecure, fearful, confused, pensive, and in some cases desperate. The increased pressures and stresses foisted upon males today is leaving them in search of true meaning.

I recently lunched with two different men in the same month who had two entirely different circumstances, but the same need. One man was 45-years-old, unemployed for the past six months, frustrated, unfulfilled, and terribly afraid. With two children in college, no income, and a high mortgage payment each month, his savings were all but depleted. His wife had been forced to return to the work place, but earned pittance in comparison to what he had earned before he was terminated. I shared Christ and several scriptures with him on God's sovereignty, on trust, on faith, and on putting Jesus first. We prayed and parted.

Later in the month I had lunch with another man in his late fifties. He owned a fairly large and successful engineering company outright. While his income was phenomenal with all the trappings of an expensive home, a weekend get away, a float plane, and a yacht, he was empty on the inside and very depressed. A strained marriage, an alienated son, and worsening diabetes combined to make him an unhappy camper. In his words, he had burned the candle at both ends and was looking for more wax!

Two men. Two extremely different circumstances. But one need—a right relationship with God through Christ. I was privileged to share with both. I pointed out to both men that receiving Christ as Savior won't solve all your problems, but it will empower you to:

...Do all things through Christ who strengthens you (Philippians 4:13).

From my perspective, we've never had a riper harvest than now. The false props of security, meaning, significance, hope, and fulfillment are crumbling fast. We need to be there, not to "pick up the pieces" but with the authentic prop, Jesus Christ, who won't crumble in tough times.

I heard that six weeks before Elvis Presley died he was interviewed by a reporter. The reporter reminded him that when his career started Elvis said he wanted three things in life; wealth, fame, and happiness. Then the reporter said, "Are you happy Elvis?" His response shocked the reporter. "No, I'm very lonely." He was rich, he was famous, but he wasn't happy.

What a picture of many men today. Men with and without money are lonely, empty, unfulfilled. All the knick-knacks of a pleasure seeking world cannot appease the deep hunger within, but Christ can! We have the answer, we hold the key.

What is your passion? Golf? Racquetball? Monday night football? Skiing? Snorkeling? Flying? Boating? Racing? Jogging? Those are all wonderful pastimes, and

as men we need some of them for variety. But I appeal to
you...make your deepest, most consistent passion the sharing with other guys what Christ has wrought in you.

These verses by Henry Crocker really say it all when it
comes to passion.

Give us a watchword for the hour,
A thrilling word, a word of power;
A battle-cry, A flaming breath
That calls to conquest or to death!

A word to rouse the church from rest,
To heed her Master's high request:
The call is given, Ye host arise,
Our watchword is "EVANGELIZE!"

The glad evangel now proclaim
Through all the earth in Jesus' name
This word is ringing through the skies,
EVANGELIZE, EVANGELIZE!

To dying men, a fallen race
Make known the gift of gospel grace,
The word that now in darkness lies
EVANGELIZE, EVANGELIZE!

Remember the race-car driver in Florida I visited? His
passion bled through, loud and clear. I believe, gentlemen,
when we "Start Our Engines," our passion for lost men
will bleed through as well! Let's do it!

10

THE HERO AT THE TRACK

A Man and His Children

Among the scores of pictures, at the Museum of Racing in Daytona Beach, one instantly caught my eye. I don't even remember the racer's name, but he was standing next to his car at the end of the race, holding a son in one arm, and another son in the other arm. The two little boys had a look on their faces I'll never forget. Both were staring into daddy's face with a look of wonderment and admiration. The caption below read, "OUR HERO!" Perfect caption. On that memorable day when their dad came in first, every sports star, entertainment star, and military hero paled in significance for those two boys.

"Johnnie," asked the kindergarten teacher, "is the world round?" "No ma'am" was the reply. "If it isn't, then I suppose it's flat," exclaimed the teacher. "No ma'am." "Well," said the teacher, "if the world isn't round and it isn't flat, then what is it?" "My dad says it's crooked," Johnnie said matter-of-factly! Be careful, dad, what you say; it will be repeated by your children!

I don't know a man who hasn't struggled with his role as a father. Often the pressures of earning a living eclipse the priority of being the kind of father God wants us to be.

The son of a prominent executive gives a description of his father as a Phi Beta Kappa, a Rhodes scholar and a company president who "flunked marriage, fatherhood, friendship, and fun." So, what does it profit a man to gain professional and monetary success, become a household word, and soar with the eagles, at the expense of his own children?

A few years back, I read the results of a poll conducted by the Wall Street Journal, coupled with a Gallop poll. They interviewed 300 chief executive officers of 1,300 large United States corporations, including 100 of the Fortune companies. Eighty percent of those polled said that their families had suffered because of their careers.

Because men are professionally driven, and inextricably connected to their work, only a few realize that their children are gifts from God. He has entrusted their care and shaping to their parents.

I heard recently that one third of America's children are not living with their natural fathers. Seventy percent of men in prison grew up without a father. Today, well over 15 million kids are growing up without any father. No one denies the fact that crime is rampant in America, 90 percent perpetrated by young men. Our government can pass a thousand $20 billion crime bills, but to no avail, until we get to the heart of the matter.

GENTLEMEN, START YOUR ENGINES IN YOUR HOME AND FOR YOUR CHILDREN!

I stood at a wind swept cemetery last year while six children watched tearlessly as the remains of their dad were lowered into a grave. I sensed tension, and noticed a definite lack of emotion, from the wife and all of the grown kids. As I was walking to my car, that cold January day, one of the sons followed me. He said one of the saddest things I've ever heard:

"We loved our dad, but he never returned the favor. He made an 'A' in building his empire, but he flunked 'Fathering 101.' That young man went on to say that if God allowed him to marry and have children, he would never neglect his children the way his father had neglected his.

Solomon said:

...and parents are the pride of their children (Proverbs 17:6b).

Yet the jolting truth is that the average father spends about one and one-half minutes PER DAY with his children. If that's average, there are hundreds of thousands of fathers who spend no time at all with their children!

I'm amazed at how many times in scripture, FATHERS are singled out for shaping and molding their children's lives.

In Deuteronomy 6:6ff - though not specifically named, by context and custom, it's clear this command was given

to fathers, not mothers, even though it's perfectly all right
for mothers to do this.

> *Hear, O Israel: The Lord our God, the Lord is one.*
> *Love the Lord your God with all your heart and with*
> *all your soul and with all your strength. These*
> *commandments that I give you today are to be upon*
> *your hearts, impress them on your children. Talk about*
> *them when you sit at home and when you walk along*
> *the road, when you lie down and when you get up. Tie*
> *them as symbols on your hands, and bind them on your*
> *foreheads. Write them on the door frames of your*
> *houses, and on your gates. (Deuteronomy 6:4-9).*

1. Psalm 78:5-6 "He decreed statutes for Jacob and
   established the law in Israel, which he commanded
   our FOREFATHERS to teach their children, so the
   next generation would know them, even the children yet to be born, and they in turn would tell
   their children."

2. Malachi 4:5-6 "I will send you the prophet Elijah
   before that great and dreadful day of the Lord
   comes. He will turn the hearts of the fathers to
   their children, and the hearts of the children to
   their fathers..."

3. Ephesians 6:4 "FATHERS, do not exasperate your
   children; instead, bring them up in the training and
   instruction of the Lord."

I once heard about a "sidewalk superintendent" who
asked three different brick layers at a construction site,
"What are you doing?" The first mason said, "I'm laying

bricks." The second replied, "I'm putting in time." But the third rose from his knees, laid down his trowel for a moment, took off his cap, and proudly said, "I'm building a cathedral!"

Ask some dads in reference to their children, "What are you doing?" Some might say, "I'm trying to keep them in clothes." Another might say, "I'm paying a horrendous grocery bill." But hopefully many dads would say, "I'm building a life."

The last time I watched the Daytona 500 on television, I noticed that at the beginning of the race, a beautiful new car, known as the "pace" car, would appear on the track. It would proudly lead the race cars once around the track for all the crowd to see, then he would quickly get out of the way. That pace car reminds me of dads. He leads in front of his child, from age zero to 18, then quickly gets out of the way so that child's race can continue.

Any man, who isn't brain dead, certainly knows that the family is in deep trouble today. In the past ten years, sinister forces have mounted an all out attack on the home, thus crippling our civilization. No nation will rise higher than the health of its homes. When you lift the curtain and peek into homes that are dysfunctional, or disintegrating, you'll find an absent, or highly ineffective father in most cases.

How can YOU as a dad "Start Your Engine" in the home so as to get an "A" on your report card in the class called "fathering?" Here are some steps:

CLEAR TIME TO BE WITH YOUR CHILDREN

Notice, I said CLEAR time. You don't just automatically have time, you have to determine, as a dad, to clear it. I know one man in our church who schedules that time in his date book to raise it a degree of importance. Since we've already stated that the average dad spends "peanuts" in the area of spending time with his children, this is where we need to start. One father takes each of his three children to lunch or breakfast every week. He will let nothing interfere with that time of bonding. It sends a clear message to his children where they rank in his scale of priorities.

Most men I know who have put in a ten or eleven hour day at the shop, or office, come home extremely tired and spent. They long for one thing, to plop down in their easy chair and unwind. The average male in America spends three hours and 45 minutes each evening watching the tube. When Monday night football is going on, make that five hours! If he could average only 30 minutes each evening with his children, what a transformation it would be!

I was recently speaking in another city and was invited to dinner in a couple's home. It was about 6:30 in the evening. The man of the house had just gotten home from a very stressful day of surgery where glitches had occurred. I could tell by his face, and his slow pace, that he was more than tired. About five minutes after his arrival, his 15-year-old son arrived home from softball practice and said, "Dad, would you throw a few balls with me?" I saw this doctor, who had been up since four o'clock in the morning pop out of his chair, grab a catcher's mitt, and bound into the front yard. He was only out there five minutes, but it was irreplaceable! It delivered a message to his son that as a father, he was committed to him. He could have easily said, "Son, it's been a long stressful day, maybe tomorrow." But he didn't. That 42-year-old doctor knew that there were no reruns in raising his son, and that to defer or postpone time spent with him until tomorrow was not an option. Lesson learned!

LET THEIR INTERESTS BE YOUR INTERESTS

I'll never forget the first Little-League game I attended for my daughter. As the game began, her eyes scanned the bleachers to see if mom and dad had come. When she spotted us, we saw the smile cross her face that said, "They really do care." There were many things I could have been doing that day, like saving my part of the city, but there was something else just as, or more, important. I needed to let my daughter know that I was affirming of her being on this team and playing.

Whether it's parent's day at school, a piano recital, a ball game, or the receiving of an award, the fact you're there delivers a huge message to your child. Make sure when your child calls, they don't get a "busy signal" from dad.

Let Your Children See That You Love Your Wife!

I remember, 30 years ago, those who taught on family issues told parents to never engage in public affection in the presence of their children. It may plant wrong ideas in their heads. Fortunately, that somewhat prudish thinking is history now. No one can measure the respect, the admiration, and the delight of a child when they see their father take the initiative and hug or kiss their mother. That living picture is worth a million words that a child might read about a husband loving his wife, like Christ loves the church.

Of course, there are other ways a man can serve his wife in the presence of his children, and that delivers a strong message that says, "Our dad really loves our mom." I remember having dinner with a young couple with two children. At the end of the dinner, the man got up, cleared the table, put down clean forks, cut a pie and served everyone. I commented, "It's good to see a man serving his family." The wife's response was, "John has done this since we were married. If we have dessert, he clears the table, and he serves the dessert. It's something his father did in his growing-up years."

What a legacy to hand down to your son! Guess what? As I watched his five-year-old watch his dad I thought "Someday when that kid is grown and married, he'll do the same thing."

LET YOUR WIFE AND FAMILY SEE YOU TAKE THE LEAD FOR SPIRITUAL DEVELOPMENT IN THE HOME

It doesn't have to be a big deal, or something grandiose. They need to see you initiate the prayer before meals. You lead the family devotions, or see that you delegate someone else in the family to do that. You initiate Christian activities and see that everyone is ready to attend. They see and hear you speak positive words about the Bible, the Church, the pastor, and the Christian life in general.

They need to hear from you the acceptable standard for dress, conduct, for stewardship and giving, for what can be watched or not watched on television, for initiating the family's schedule. You need to be the one that sets the parameters for what your children see at movies, what they read, where they go, and their language.

MAKE SURE YOU ARE APPROACHABLE BY YOUR CHILDREN

Sometimes even dads that stay home a lot aren't approachable to their children. Here is a good list of questions to find out if you're approachable.

- Do my kids feel free to come to me with any problem?
- When they've broken something, are they afraid to tell me?
- Do I tend to explode when they have disobeyed?

- Do they know I have unconditional love for them, even when they deeply disappoint me?
- Are they afraid of me?
- Do they see me as a tiger ready to attack?
- Am I in the habit of putting them down?
- How often have I said, "I don't have time now...maybe later?"
- Do I excessively say, "Talk to your mom about that."
- Do they know my arms are a safe harbor for them?

I vividly remember going to the jail to talk to a 19-year-old young man in trouble. I made the mistake of saying to him, "Your heavenly Father can help you..." He exploded and yelled, "I want nothing to do with any father." He had measured God the Father by what he saw in his own father, a man who had no time for him, who was extremely critical of him, a man who beat him, and told him that he would never amount to anything. In his mind, anyone with the name "father" was bad news. It dawned on me for the first time in my life that my children's concept of God the Father will be gleaned from what they saw in me as a father.

In the 70's a song by Harry Chapin hit the charts, "Cat's in the Cradle." I would love to know his heart when he wrote these words;

My child arrived just the other day.
He came to the world in the usual way.
But there were planes to catch and bills to pay.
He learned to walk while I was away.
And he was talkin 'fore I knew it and as he grew,

He'd say "I'm gonna be like you, Dad,
You know I'm gonna be like you."

And the cat's in the cradle and the silver spoon.
Little boy blue and the man in the moon.
"When you comin' home Dad?"
"I don't know when, but we'll get together then,
You know we'll have a good time then."

My son turned ten just the other day.
He said, "Thanks for the ball, dad, come on let's play.
Can you teach me to throw?"
I said, "Not today, I got a lot to do."
He said, "that's O.K."
And he walked away, but his smile never dimmed
And said, "I'm gonna be like him, yeah
You know I'm gonna be like him."

And the cat's in the cradle and the silver spoon.
Little boy blue and the man in the moon.
"When you comin home, Dad?"
"I don't know when, but we'll get together then,
You know we'll have a good time then."

Well, he came home from college just the other day
So much like a man I just had to say
"Son, I'm proud of you; can't you sit for awhile?
"He shook his head and said with a smile,
"What I'd really like, Dad, is to borrow the car keys.
See you later, can I have them please?"

And the cat's in the cradle, and the silver spoon.
Little boy blue and the man in the moon.
"When you comin home son?"
"I don't know when, but we'll get together then, Dad.
You know we'll have a good time then."

I've long since retired. My son's moved away.
I called him up just the other day.
I said, "I'd like to see you if you don't mind."
He said, "I'd love to dad, if I can find the time.
You see my new job's a hassle
And the kids have the flu.
But it's sure nice talking to you, Dad,
It's been sure nice talking to you."

And I hung up the phone it occurred to me...
He'd grown up, just like me.
My boy was just like me!

And the cat's in the cradle and the silver spoon.
Little boy blue and the man in the moon.
"When you comin' home son?"
"I don't know when, but we'll get together then.
You know we'll have a good time then." [5]

If you feel the emotion reading this, that I'm feeling writing it, your eyes are moist.

Dad, whether your children are still home, or grown and gone, they're so important. If they are home, their molding and shaping years are still at your disposal. You only have a short window of time to make a mark on their lives. When that time is up, your shaping and influencing days are over.

Maybe that is why this poem, whose author is unknown, grips my heart so tightly.

"Walk a little plainer, Daddy
Said a little boy so frail,
I'm following in your footsteps,
And I don't want to fail.

Sometimes your steps are very plain,
Sometimes they're hard to see,
So walk a little plainer, Daddy
For you are leading me.

I know that once you walked this way,
Many years ago,
And what you did along the way,
I'd really like to know.
For sometimes when I am tempted
I don't know what to do
So walk a little plainer, Daddy

For I must follow you.
Someday when I'm grown up,
You are like I want to be,
Then I will have a little boy
Who will want to follow me.
And I would want to lead him right
And help him to be true,
So walk a little plainer, Daddy
For we must follow you!

Frightening? Yes. Reality? For sure. Challenging? To the core!

Gentlemen, "Start Your Engines" in the home, you're someone's hero, and they're watching you closely.

11

THOSE UNFORGIVING WALLS

A Man and His Failures

On our tour of the Daytona International Speedway, you could tell our tour guide, who doubled as the van driver, was bringing the tour to a conclusion. We were headed back to where we had started at the front gate, when he left the main track. He drove to the perimeter road, adjacent to the thick concrete wall that surrounded the whole raceway. We had seen the pits, the track itself, the warm-up area, the starting line, the finish line, the stands, but there was one more thing...he called it the wall of death. He stopped the van and we got out to stand next to this fortress of concrete. His lecture continued. He asked us all to look over the wall and back into it. We saw chips and nicks in the wall, along with some red and yellow paint. He pointed out with solemnity that it was here that one of the race car drivers met his death the year before. Then, repeating what he had said to 15 other tour groups that day and nearly 200 groups

135

that week, he broke the silence with this. "Did this driver meet his death here because they made the curves too severe? Was it because the wall was too hard? Was it because their cars were unsafe? Was the track wet and slippery? Did the driver not know what the maximum speed was to make the turn safely? NO! It was none of those. He broke the rules, exceeded the safe speed, did the foolish thing, and left behind a young wife and two darling little boys. He ignored the fact that these walls are unforgiving."

There was dead silence as our group of 12 felt with our fingers the chipped out places in the wall, and even saw small bits and pieces of debris from the crash. My mind was "racing" with thoughts of that man's wife and children who must go on and face life without a husband and dad. It all seemed so unnecessary, so senseless, so tragic.

I also began to think about something else. God has placed some impenetrable walls around our lives and, they too, are unforgiving. Those walls cut us no slack. They're not elastic. They won't bend, stretch, or accommodate in any way our foolishness and lack of discipline. They are amazingly hard, and if we hit them, we pay the piper, then live (or die) with our choice.

Secular guys call these walls the principles of life. They are summed up in the Bible as the Ten Commandments. They're not the ten suggestions, or the ten tips, or the ten recommendations, but the ten COMMANDMENTS. You can read them in Exodus 20, where God said what he meant, and meant what he said. If we violate them, abuse

them, or break them in our life, the consequences
are nasty.

Those commandments speak of revering God, having
no idols in our life, not taking God's name lightly, honor-
ing God's special day, respecting our parents and other
family members, and refusing to murder, commit adultery, steal, lie, or covet. He has placed these around our
lives, not to rob us of a good time, or to be a party-pooper.
He has done it for our protection and well-being. To ignore, or attempt to break those walls with fast living will
certainly be to our peril.

The Bible says it well:

> *Do not be deceived, God cannot be mocked. A man
> reaps what he sows. The one who sows to please his
> sinful nature, from that nature will reap
> destruction...(Galatians 6:7-8).*

What kind of harvest do you want later in your life?
It better be from the crop that you're sowing now, or
you'll hit hard those unforgiving walls.

Here are a few "walls" we men are in constant danger
of hitting, and I mention them only so we can avoid them
at all costs.

WALLS OF THE TONGUE

We men really struggle with this. I've heard it said
of men who come to Christ that their mouth and tongue
are the last to get converted! I think that's true. Solomon
knew how prone we are to "hit the wall" with our tongues.

That's why he wrote:

> *He who guards his lips guards his life, but he who speaks rashly will come to ruin (Proverbs 13:3).*

The idea of "guarding" our lips means that we're to set a sentinel over them, so that we weigh carefully what comes out. Have you ever stopped to think what kind of words we're capable of speaking?

Harsh words
Bitter words
Condemning words
Accusing words
Angry words
Blaming words
Cursing words
Critical words
Judgmental words
Inaccurate words
Inflammatory words
Gossiping Words
Vulgar words
Arrogant words
Cynical words

Or...
Pleasant words
Healing words
Helpful words
Compassionate words

Upbuilding words
Creative words
Assuring words
Encouraging words
Pure words
Appreciative words
Complimentary words
Edifying words
It's no wonder that the wise king also said:

The tongue has the power of life and death...(Proverbs 18:21a).

In one sense we can create life or cause death with our tongues.

What kind of words are you using when you speak to your wife? Your children? Your neighbors? The people at your work? To strangers? How many times a day are you saying, "thank you very much," or "I really appreciate that?" Indeed,

Pleasant words are a honeycomb, sweet to the soul and healing to the bones (Proverbs 16:24).

Are you speaking with a clean tongue? Do you still have foul language around others? The best description of the kind of speech God wants for us is seen in Colossians 4:

Let your conversation be always full of grace, seasoned with salt, so that you may know how to answer everyone (Colossians 4:6).

When we violate this, we "hit the wall" and it will return to haunt us.

Your Thoughts And Vision

What do you spend a lot of time thinking about? What are your fantasies? What do you watch? We're told again and again to have the mind of Christ, and that we tend to become what dominates our thought life. God's perimeter wall around our life is usually violated first by our thought life. All anger, strife, sexual immorality, and vulgar speech begin with what we're thinking. That's why we're encouraged in scripture to have the mind of Christ. Paul listed a group of virtues in Philippians dealing with what is true, noble, right, pure, lovely, admirable, excellent, praiseworthy, then he said, "THINK ABOUT SUCH THINGS" (Philippians 4:8). No doubt we could conquer our actions if we first conquered our thought life. Maybe that's why Paul wrote:

> ...we take captive every thought to make it obedient to Christ (2 Corinthians 10:5).

As a man thinks, so is he. We really do become the sum total of what dominates our thought life.

Now what about your eyes? What do you look at? What do you focus on? Here God has set limits also. Jesus gave us a firm warning:

> You have heard that it was said, "Do not commit adultery." But I tell you that anyone who LOOKS at a woman lustfully has already committed adultery with her in his heart (Matthew 5:27-28).

Notice how Jesus raised the standard of the old law instead of lowering it. He was saying, "You've read that the ACT of sexual immorality is wrong, but I'm telling you that you can perform the act with your eyes." Are you guarding the eyegate of your life, men? Solomon had some very good advice when it came to lusting after other women with our eyes.

Put away perversity from your mouth; keep corrupt talk from your lips. Let your eyes look straight ahead, fix your gaze directly before you (Proverbs 4:24, 25).

Notice, in two short verses, he mentions our mouth, our lips, and our gaze, our eyes. Biblical characters were realists. They struggled with the very same temptations we struggle with. Job was one who obviously struggled with the temptation to look at beautiful women. He nipped it in the right place.

I made a covenant with my eyes not to look lustfully at a girl (Job 31:1).

Good move, Job! David wasn't so fortunate. One evening when he was on his roof top he noticed a beautiful woman taking a bath. It was Bathsheba, whose husband was off to war. David couldn't resist. Someone has accurately said that David went through a series of steps:

- He looked
- He lusted
- He laid
- He lied

Those are the descending steps of death! It all began with a thought that was soon translated to a look, which stirred lust, and in turn ended in a moment of sexual passion. David hit the wall, and oh, how he paid again and again for his sin. We will too. A Sunday School children's song has one verse that says:

> Be careful little eyes what you see,
> Be careful little eyes what you see,
> For the Father up above is looking down in love,
> So be careful little eyes what you see.

It's not just little eyes that need to be careful. Never has the use of pornography been more blatant than now. Many men have a little secret that their wives and their kids don't know about. They view pornography. It is a multi-billion dollar business in this country. Some men are hooked on it, and can't break away. I had a pastor of an evangelical church come to me only three years ago to say that he visits the porn shops at least three times per week, and it all started with a casual look. Unfortunately for him, it didn't stop there. Fearful that he might have AIDS or some other horrible sexually transmitted disease, he walked into my office to give up. It tore his whole family apart, he lost his marriage of 15 years, and had to leave his church in shame and degradation. It took months of treatment for his syphilis to heal, but fortunately he didn't have AIDS.

YOUR BODY

Pollsters disagree on the number of men who are sexually unfaithful to their wives in marriage. Some place it as low as 30 percent while more recent polls indicate that nearly 50 percent of men have extra-marital affairs. This means a large number of men "color outside the lines" when it comes to marital fidelity. They "hit the wall." It's a very expensive hit.

Scripture tells us that our bodies are nothing less that the temple of the Holy Spirit. God has ordained them as the buildings that house the Holy Spirit. The Holy Spirit's address is our body (I Corinthians 3:16). It goes on to say:

> *If anyone destroys God's temple, God will destroy him, for God's temple is sacred, and you are that temple (I Corinthians 3:17).*

Those are strong words, and we ought to stand before them with fear and trembling. What about it guys, are you keeping your body pure? We've already seen in chapter four how a clean carburetor can make the difference in a race. The power of a clean body can make the difference for us as well.

The best advice I can give you to keep you from hitting the wall at this point are the words of Solomon:

> *Drink water from your own cistern, running water from your own well. Should your springs overflow into the streets, your streams of water in the public squares? Let them be yours alone, never to be shared with strangers. May your fountain be blessed, and may you rejoice in the wife of your youth...may her breasts satisfy you always, may you ever be captivated by her love. Why be captivated, my son, by an adulteress? Why embrace the bosom of another man's wife? (Proverbs 5:15-17, 19b-20).*

Good advice.

I'll call him "Tom." The name is fictitious, but the story is real. Faithfully married for 12 years, Tom took a new job with a financial research company. Still a handsome man at 33-years-old, he met Tonya, a receptionist. At first it was a friendship, then occasional lunches together where Tom confided that he wasn't being sexually gratified by his wife. Tonya, a recent divorcee, shared how very lonely her nights were, so the inevitable happened. Both "happened" to be working late one night to get ready for a seminar. Tonya complained of a stiff neck. Tom began to massage her neck, which led to other things. By ten o'clock in the evening, behind Tom's desk with the lights out, he flushed 12 years of fidelity down the drain. Worse, the affair continued until Tom's wife was tipped off by a fellow employee. When she confronted Tom, he broke down, and in tears he admitted the whole thing.

His wife was a lovely, Christian woman, and though deeply hurt, extended her forgiveness to him. In less than three weeks, Tom was with Tonya again, and the whole saga resumed! He lost his marriage, his two children's respect, his job, and eventually his health. That's when he came to me, a broken man. I'll never forget his words. "My whole life shattered for a few minutes of sexual pleasure outside my marriage." I prayed and ministered God's Word to him, but his life was shattered. I never saw him again. How many "Toms" are out there with the same tragic story, because they "hit the wall" with an uncontrolled body.

Maybe you're saying, "I've done that in the past, is there any hope for me?" Yes. Rest in God's gracious forgiveness (I John 1:9), and learn to set your minds on things that are above (Colossians 3:1). Though you've blown it by immorality, there is healing and forgiveness in God's abundant grace. Go and sin no more!

Your tongue, your mind...and your body. Don't hit the wall with them, or someone will be looking at the scars and asking, "Why?"

> Do you not know that in a race all the runners run, but only one gets the prize? Run is such a way as to get the prize. Everyone who competes in the games goes into strict training. They do it to get a crown that will not last, but we do it to get a crown that will last forever (I Corinthians 9:24-25).

12

THE FLAG AT THE FINISH

The Score at the End of Your Life

In racing, the finish line is the bottom line. It doesn't matter whether you've been racing two years or twenty years...or if you've spent $30,000 on your car or $70,000...it doesn't matter how bright and shiny your car is, or if it's painted blue, red, or yellow...or how proficient your engine is or isn't...whether your name is a household word or you're the new kid on the block. It doesn't matter whether it's your first race or fiftieth...there is only one thing that counts...WHEN AND HOW YOU CROSSED THE FINISH LINE. Everything else pales by comparison.

So it is with life. When you get to the finish line, it's not important how famous you are, how rich you are, how many titles you hold, or whether the car that got you there is a Ford or Rolls Royce.

Most men I know don't think much about the finish line, yet we'll all cross it. The last time I checked the death ratio in America it was still one per person. No one will escape the grim reaper. We have a rendezvous with death, and its date has been set. The Bible speaks of our "allotted months" coming to an end (Job 21:21). God has the day of your death circled on his calendar, and he isn't telling you when it is. All of us are one heartbeat away from eternity. Everything you did in your life that could be called success pales in significance if you're not ready to cross the finish line.

Life is short. It is also fragile. James, in his epistle, describes life from the cradle to the grave like this:

> What is your life? You are a mist that appears for a little while and then vanishes (James 4:14).

I recently read part of a speech by a man who retired at 70 years old. At the end of the short speech, he said, as he brushed the tears back, "The trip is incredibly short." He's right. It's like the day of the race. The trips around the track fly by, and the finish flag comes all too soon, but come it does.

So, when you cross the finish line of life, there will be some questions that we will inevitably ask. How will YOU answer these questions?

DID I GIVE LIFE MY BEST?

My father didn't become a Christian until later in his life, but he taught me some valuable things growing up. One of the most valuable was this, "Son, whatever you do, give it your best, if you don't, you'll live with the regrets for a long time." He was right. Read the question again. I didn't say give life THE best, but MY best. We're not competing against others. God wants to make sure when we come to finish line, we can look back and honestly say, "I gave it my best...my best energy, my best time, my best ability." Are you living up to the potential God put within you? Are you giving your best to your wife, your kids, your job, your church? Jesus did all things well, and so should we.

DID I MAKE THE MAIN THING–THE MAIN THING?

That may sound like double talk, but it's really asking, "Will I cross the finish line with my priorities in the right order?" Did I give my first allegiance to the things that matter? What are the things that matter most? The first priority of our lives should be commitment to Jesus Christ:

> But seek first his kingdom and his righteousness...(Matthew 6:33).

Next come your wife and family. If you happen to be a woman reading this, it's your husband and children. A woman can live without a lot of things in her marriage, but she cannot live without knowing where she stands in her husband's pecking-order of priorities. If she's behind your job, your golf, your television, your hobbies, and your other friends, your priorities are out of kilter.

I stood at a cemetery recently, and on virtually every tombstone I saw two dates. The first was the year of

birth, and the second was the year of death. Between the
two dates was a small dash. I wondered what that dash rep-
resented for so many. Did they make the main thing the main
thing, or did they spend their lives majoring on minors, high-
lighting the insignificant and the unimportant? The old
maxim is still true: "Only one life, twill soon be past; only
what's done for Christ will last." Jesus said:

> As long as it is day, we must do the work of him who
> sent me. Night is coming when no one can work (John
> 9:4).

There was an urgency in those words. Jesus viewed
life as a window of time, so short, so fleeting, that we
need to give it our best shot by devoting our highest energy to eternal issues, not just issues that deal with time.

I recently attended a time-management and adminis-
tration seminar. The very first message on the large screen
was: NO ONE EVER CAME TO THE END OF THEIR
LIFE WITH THE REGRET THAT THEY DIDN'T
SPEND MORE TIME AT THE OFFICE!

Of all examples of people who made the main thing
the main thing, Paul stands at the top of the list. One day
on the road to Damascus, he was blinded by a great light,
and he heard a voice. He was stopped cold in his tracks.
He was converted to Christ. From that moment on, Paul's
whole life was a magnificent obsession, and that obsession was Christ. He slept, ate, lived, and breathed to make
Christ known. Perhaps that is why at the end of his life,
he wrote the words I hope I can say at the end of my life.

I have fought the good fight, I have finished the race, I have kept the faith (2 Timothy 4:7).

Paul could actually say he finished his life. Many begin, few finish, they simply quit. A man's priorities should be in this order:

- Personal relationship with Jesus Christ
- Commitment to wife and children
- Your job
- Your hobbies and recreation

Make sure that the dash between the dates represents more than just the a number of years you breathed.

ARE ALL ACCOUNTS SETTLED?

Are all differences settled? Has all animosity melted? Are all grudges released?

One of the saddest things I've ever seen was a death scene in a hospital. A man lay dying who had not spoken to one of his sons for over seven years. He was a farmer, and the grievance was over 50 head of cattle that the son claimed the father had given him, but the father claimed that he had loaned to his son. Earlier it had gone to court, but a judge threw the case out, refusing to get embroiled in a family dispute. The son kept the cattle, and the father became embittered to the point of cutting the son out of his will. When it became evident that the older man was dying, I, along with his wife, pleaded with him to call for the son. He refused. Finally the son came to see his father, but the old man refused to speak to, or even look at him. While the son waited in the lobby, the nurse came to say that the man had expired. It was as if knife had been driven through his son. There were no reruns, no second chances. A man died harboring a grudge against his own blood son. This is why we need to keep all of our accounts short, or better still, nonexistent.

A young man in our church used to drive an ambulance. He told me of an occasion where they were called to a head-on collision. One victim was very critical, pinned by the steering column and not able to breathe. The ambulance driver said they could hear him saying, "I forgive you, Ann, I forgive you, please know I forgive you." Ann was his wife, and they had been estranged for almost a year due to an affair she had had. Though she broke up with her lover, and asked this man's forgiveness, he had refused to forgive, or to have her back.

Now that he was staring death in the face, this was all he could think about. Unfortunately, Ann never got to hear his words, except secondhand. The man died shortly after they got him to the hospital.

Make sure you have no regrets at sunset. Do whatever you have to do to clear the air on your personal relationships. In Ephesians, Paul said:

> Do not let the sun go down while you are still angry, and do not give the devil a foothold (Ephesians 4:26-27).

I'm sure he meant, on a day by day basis, to make sure you clear all offenses. The fact is that one day will come in your life when the sun will go down permanently.

AM I PREPARED TO CROSS THE FINISH LINE?

Maybe a better word would be qualified. Am I qualified to cross the finish line? I don't have to be perfect to cross. I don't have to be a renown theologian or hold theology degrees, but I do have to be spiritually qualified. What qualifies me to cross?

a) *Admitting that I'm a sinner.* Romans 3:23 says that "...all have sinned and fall short of the glory of God."

b) *Realize that sin has separated you from a holy God.* The Bible says in Isaiah 59:2, "...your iniquities have separated you from your God..." It also says, "For the wages of sin is death..."(Romans 6:23). That is a spiritual death that renders us insensitive to God.

c) *You cannot do anything to remove sin from your life.* The Bible says, "Although you wash yourself with soda and use an abundance of soap, the stain of your guilt is still before me, declares the Sovereign Lord" (Jeremiah 2:22). Because we are spiritually bankrupt, we cannot come up with what it takes to purchase our salvation.

d) *Know that Jesus Christ is God's answer to your sin!* His death on the cross became full payment for the guilt of our sin. Jesus said, "I am the way and the truth and the life. No man comes to the Father except through me" (John 14:6).

e) *You must RECEIVE Christ to be saved.* We're told
to "believe in the Lord Jesus, and you will be
saved..."(Acts 26:31). We also receive him by confessing him to be Lord with our lips. "...if you confess with your mouth, 'Jesus is Lord,' and believe
in your heart that God raised him from the dead,
you will be saved." (Romans 10:9) We receive
Christ by calling on his name. "Everyone who calls
on the name of the Lord will be saved" (Romans
10:13). If you have never done that, a good way
to pray is:

*Dear God, I know that I'm a sinner. I'm sorry for my
sin. Lord Jesus, come into my heart right now. I receive
you as my personal Savior, and believe that You died on
the cross and rose again from the dead. Amen.*

Though the implications of all of the above would fill
volumes, the simple truth is that only those who believe in
Jesus and have invited him into their hearts are truly qualified to cross the finish line.

Have you received Christ? Do you know for SURE
that if you died tonight you would go to heaven?

A Persian fable tells about a court jester who alone
could make the old king laugh. When the king would feel
blue and discouraged, he would call the jester to lighten
his cares. The king gave the jester a stick and told him,
"When you find a bigger fool than yourself, give him this
stick." One day the king became very ill. He called for his
jester to cheer him up. Upon arriving, the king said to the

jester, "O jester, cheer me up because I'm going on a long journey." "Where art thou going?" the jester asked. "On a long, long journey," the king responded. "Hast thou made preparation for thy journey, O king?" "No, I've made none." The jester reached inside his cloak and pulled out the stick the king had given him years before. "Here, O king, is the stick. I trifle with the things of time, but you have trifled with the things of eternity. You are a bigger fool than I."

Nothing else matters in life unless you're ready to cross the finish line.

Gentlemen, "Start Your Engines." The race has begun!

What Kind Of Legacy Will I Leave Behind?

When the finish flag is waved over my life, I want to leave my children and grandchildren a worthwhile legacy. I'm not talking about money, stocks, and real estate. I'm talking about character, a godly life, and faith in the finished work of Christ. Listen to these words Paul wrote to young Timothy:

> *I have been reminded of your sincere faith, which first lived in your grandmother Lois, and in your mother Eunice and, I am persuaded, now lives in you (2 Timothy 1:5).*

What a legacy those two mothers left, the grandmother to her daughter, and the daughter to her son. That's called passing the torch. I love the song, "May Those Who Come

Behind Us Find us Faithful." What will you leave your children? What will be left is really determined by what consumes your life right now.

13

GENTLEMEN, START YOUR ENGINES - NOW!

A Man and His Determination

I'll call him Clyde. Thirty-eight, handsome, wavy dark hair, he was wearing a beautiful silk-blend teal suit, flashing eyes, and a ring on his right hand studded with larger-than-usual diamonds. We met at his request at a very classy restaurant overlooking the Puget Sound.

Clyde's first words to me were, "Bob, I'm in deep, deep trouble!" I found out that Clyde was just like my car. Just about everything that could be wrong with it was; electrical system, bad muffler, out of alignment, out of tune, and burning excessive oil! Where do you start?

Clyde went to a well know university at 19 and sowed an abundance of wild oats. Because of his good looks, and his money (his father had an endless supply), Clyde never wanted for a date. He confessed to me that he had had probably 30 different sexual "conquests" before he was married at 24, including his fiancee who became his wife.

Within a year of his marriage, he did a foolish thing. He got involved with a 20-year-old secretary at his office and, at the ripe old age of 25, Clyde found himself divorced, living with his new flame. She was soon pregnant, and when he attempted to ditch her, by paying her off, her father filed a law suit against him and won. He's was still paying for that child's support. He was also paying child support for his ex-wife's child, born four months after their marriage.

Though an executive in his father's company, Clyde's finances were running low. He married a second time, only to commit the same mistakes he made in his first marriage, so divorce number two became a reality. At 34, Clyde married again, this time to a woman with two children.

That marriage was the topic of our luncheon. His wife was fed up with his drinking, his gambling, his infidelity, his violence (a relatively new development), and his total lack of sensitivity to her and her children. He had been served with papers only the day before we met for lunch. In his words, "I need this thing fixed and fixed fast!" But what Clyde needed was to start over again.

We ate quickly, then headed for the waterfront to watch the ships come and go. Three hours later, in brokenness, Clyde restarted his engines, and made a recommitment of his life in many areas.

- Personal holiness
- Restoring his devotional quiet times
- Recommitments to his marriage as a man of God
- Abandoning all gambling, drinking, swearing, X-rated shows, other women, etc.
- Church attendance weekly
- Accountability and discipleship group

I'm happy to say, that when we left that waterfront park, his engine was purring like a kitten with regards to what needed to be done in each of these areas and, thanks to a group of men, Clyde is to this day, still on course, and is rebuilding his marriage.

This book has really had only one theme: IT'S TIME FOR US MEN TO "START OUR ENGINES." The ball is your court. Yours is the next move. You're asking, "How do I get started, practically?" I'm glad you asked! The following is a sequential step-by-step plan.

Start Your Engine Today, Not Tomorrow!

Don't say, "Well, there are some things I need to get in place..." No, start today or you won't start at all! No postponing, no deferring, no excuses. It's now or never.

Begin By Developing A Consistent Quiet Time In Your Life.

Your engine will sputter, knock, and eventually quit if this isn't in place. I refer you back to chapter one for tools. Remember Mark 1:35. If Jesus found the necessary time for a time alone with God, to be in His Word and pray on a DAILY basis, certainly you won't even get to the starting line without it, much less finish the race.

START A KILLING PLAN TODAY!

Sounds awful, doesn't it? But I'm referring to what Paul exhorted us to do in Colossians:

> PUT TO DEATH, therefore, whatever belongs to earthly nature...(Colossians 3:5).

He then goes on to list 12 horrible habits men acquire that need to go, be killed, be decimated. You might just want to take a whole day of prayer and fasting. Write out your sins on a sheet of paper, and then cut them in two as a symbol of being finished with them.

PRACTICE ANY RESTITUTION THAT NEEDS TO HAPPEN

Engines won't run long if they are clogged with grimy grudges, animosities, unsettled accounts, wrongs that need to be righted by you, and maybe even money that needs to be paid back. Zaccheus, upon conversion, decided to pay back four times what he had extorted from others. Whatever you decide to do, under God's direction, will be good. Don't leave this important step out, or your engine won't run well, if it even runs at all.

REDEDICATE YOURSELF TO YOUR WIFE AND CHILDREN

Reaffirm your love for her, ask her forgiveness if you've done anything to impair the relationship. Clean the slate. Let her know you're going to be constantly making a concerted effort to carry out your role in marriage, which is loving her like Christ loves the church. Let your children know that you're recommitting yourself to them: to spend more time, to understand them more, to invest in their lives what only a father can invest.

REDEDICATE YOUR WORK TO GOD AND YOUR BOSS

In keeping with Colossians 3:23, let the Lord know that from this point on, you're working for Him. Let your boss know, from that same verse, that if in the past all of you hasn't been put into your work, it will from here on out. From now on you'll work at it with all your heart. Most men spend about 50 hours, out of 178 hours in a week (a sizable chunk!) working for a living. That's almost one-third of a man's entire week! Make a decision that you'll no longer gripe, complain, whine, or become an irritant on the job, but that you will work with joy and a positive attitude.

RE-DEDICATE YOUR LIFE TO YOUR PASTOR AND CHURCH

Your pastor is the shepherd over your soul. Respect him or get in a church whose pastor you do respect. He's keeping watch over you and will have to give an account to God (Hebrews 13:17). No, he's not perfect, he makes many mistakes, but he needs your friendship, your love, and your support. You may need to make an appointment with him just to let him know you're making this new beginning in your life.

Become involved not only in consistent church attendance, but in serving Christ in some ministry. Whether it's ushering, singing in the choir, driving the church bus, or serving on a committee. Don't be just a "consumer," be a "producer" in your local church.

MAKE A NEW START AS SALT AND LIGHT!

I know you've read chapter nine on having a passion for lost men. I think you need to let God know that you're available to talk to other men about their relationship to Christ even if it's just sharing your own personal testimony, and what God has done for you. You have neighbors, friends, relatives, work colleagues to whom you've never borne a witness. Rededicate yourself to a renewed effort to touch those people by being salt, which flavors, and light, which dispels darkness.

RECONSECRATE YOUR MONEY TO GOD

In chapter six, we established that most men are driven by the purse. In too many instances it isn't man making the money, it's money making the man. Re-read Luke 14:33 where Jesus made it clear that we must renounce all ownership or we can't be His disciple. Renouncing ownership doesn't mean we have a disdain for money, it just means we concede that we own nothing, and that God owns everything. He has called us to be managers of what belongs to Him.

You need to take your wallet and checkbook, get on your knees, and hold them up to the Lord, saying,

> *"God I re-consecrate this to You. This is Yours, not mine, and I'm starting all over today with a renewed effort to be a good manager: how I earn it, how I save it, how I spend it, and how I give it."*

If money has a hold on you, release it to God. If your priorities aren't right in this department of your life, they won't be in any other.

REDEDICATE YOURSELF TO YOUR FRIENDS, OLD AND NEW

I refer you to chapter five, THOSE RACING BUDDIES. If there is any place we need to "Start Our Engines," it's in the area of our friendships. Where are your friendships going? Are you affecting your friends positively for Christ? Are you keeping any friendships that tend to deteriorate your holiness?

I'm not suggesting that you keep no non-Christian friends. Otherwise how would you ever win them to Christ?

Like Clyde, you too can start life over, beginning right now!

After working with men over the years I have found myself praying a prayer I've penned—praying for a new breed of men that will make a difference in our world:

GOD GIVE US MEN!

God, give us men...ribbed with the steel of Your Spirit who will not flinch when the battle is fierce...who won't acquiesce at the bargaining table or compromise in principle; Give us men who won't retreat on the battle field...men who won't sell out for lucre or convenience. God, give us men who won't be bought, bartered, or badgered by the enemy...men who will go the distance, pay the price, suffer the loss...make the sacrifice...stand the ground...and hold high the torch of conviction in the face of pressure.

God, give us men obsessed with principle instead of pleasure, committed to truth instead of ease; give us men true to your word, stripped of self-seeking with their yen for security...men who will pay the high price of freedom...and go any lengths for truth. God give us men delivered from mediocrity, men with vision high, pride low, faith wide, love deep, and patience long...men who will dare to march to the drumbeat of a different drummer, men who will not surrender right for a mess of pottage, or run from trials and evade conflict. God, give us men more interested in scars instead of medals, work instead of leisure, challenge instead of easy projects, and in winning instead of just a tie.

Give us men who will give their lives for the highest, who are fearless in the face of danger, calm in the midst of criticism, and courageous in the presence of the enemy. Give us men who will pray earnestly, work long, preach clearly, fight bravely, love ridiculously, and wait patiently...give us men whose strength is equal to their task...men who won't fade under the fierce searchlight of criticism, or fear at the shouting of the opposition, who won't bend under the heavy load of responsibility. Lord, give us men...willing to be a minority, to stand for the unpopular cause, who can perform without being stroked, thanked, awarded or promoted. Give us men willing to forfeit personal preference for the higher cause, personal rights for deeper responsibilities, and convenient comfort for consecrated convictions. Give us men who, when the battle is done, the dust has settled, and the victory announced, will stand tall, unafraid, unashamed and say, "it was well worth it."

God...give us men!

NOTES:

[1] Steve Farrar, "Real Men Don't," in Bill McCartney, *What Makes a Man*, Navpress, 1992, p. 80.

[2] Arthur Guiterman, "Dug From The Mountainside," in Robert J. Hastings, *My Money and My God*, Broadman Press, 1961, p. 79.

[3] Mazie V. Caruthers, "The Prayer of Any Husband," in James Dalton Morrison (ed.), *Masterpieces of Religious Verse*, Harper and Brothers Publishers, 1948, p. 335.

[4] Edgar Guest, "Myself," in James Dalton Morrison (ed.), *Masterpieces of Religious Verse*, Harper and Brothers Publishers, 1948, p. 286.

[5] Harry and Sandy Chapin, Lyrics from "Cats in the Cradle," 1974 Story Songs, LTD., New York, Used with permission. All rights reserved.

Bob Moorehead, Ph.D., is the senior pastor of Overlake Christian Church in Kirkland, Washington. He and Glenita, his wife of over thirty years, have three children. Dr. Moorehead has authored a total of nine books including: *Before You Throw in the Towel, The Marriage Repair Kit, The Husband Handbook,* and *How to Counsel Yourself and Others from the Bible.*

Other books and publications by Bob Moorehead:

Before You Throw in the Towel

Counsel Yourself and Others From the Bible

Courageous Christianity

Free At Last

God's Cure for Depression

Help, I've Been Cheated On

Give Me One Good Reason

Real Answers to Life's Problems

The Growth Factor

The Marriage Repair Kit

The Unpardonable Sin

The Husband Handbook

Cover Design:
Kelly A. Smith

Printing and Binding:
Versa Press, Inc.
East Peoria, Illinois